From The Nation's #1 Educational Publisher K-12

Grade 3

Enrichment Reading

CONTENTS

Following Directions 3

Getting the Main Idea 4

Getting the Main Idea 5

Drawing Conclusions 6

Drawing Conclusions 7

Identifying Inferences 8

Identifying Inferences 9

Getting the Main Idea 10

Getting the Main Idea 11

Getting the Facts 12

Getting the Facts 13

Following Directions 14

Using the Context 15

Getting the Main Idea 16

Getting the Main Idea 17

Drawing Conclusions 18

Drawing Conclusions 19

Detecting the Sequence 20

Detecting the Sequence 21

Getting the Main Idea 22

Getting the Main Idea 23

Progress Check 24

Progress Check 25

Identifying Inferences 26

Identifying Inferences 27

Getting the Main Idea 28

Getting the Main Idea 29

Drawing Conclusions 30

Drawing Conclusions 31

Getting the Facts 32

Getting the Facts 33

Progress Check 34

Using the Context 35

Getting the Main Idea 36

Getting the Main Idea 37

Detecting the Sequence 38

Detecting the Sequence 39

Drawing Conclusions 40

Drawing Conclusions 41

Getting the Main Idea 42

Getting the Main Idea 43

Following Directions 44

Using the Context 45

Identifying Inferences 46

Identifying Inferences 47

Getting the Main Idea 48

Getting the Main Idea 49

Drawing Conclusions 50

Drawing Conclusions 51

Getting the Facts 52

Getting the Facts 53

Following Directions 54

Using the Context 55

Getting the Main Idea 56

Getting the Main Idea 57

Detecting the Sequence 58

Detecting the Sequence 59

Drawing Conclusions 60

Drawing Conclusions 61

Identifying Inferences 62

Identifying Inferences 63

Progress Check 64

Answer Key 65

Credits:
Authors
Richard A. Boning
William H. Wittenberg

McGraw-Hill Consumer Products Editorial/Production Team
Vincent F. Douglas, B.S. and M. Ed.
Tracy R. Paulus
Jennifer P. Blashkiw

Cover Design & Illustration: Beachcomber Studio

McGraw-Hill
Consumer Products
A Division of The *McGraw-Hill* Companies

Send all inquires to:
McGraw-Hill Consumer Products
250 Old Wilson Bridge Road
Worthington, Ohio 43085

1-57768-443-5   1 2 3 4 5 6 7 8 9 10 QPD 04 03 02 01 00 99

FOLLOWING DIRECTIONS

Read each set of directions, then circle the letter choice that best answers the question about the directions.

DIRECTIONS

Fly a kite in an open spot far from electric power lines. Never use metal wire or wet string. If your kite gets caught in a power line or in tree branches near a power line, don't try to get it down. Instead, call your electric power company.

---

1. This tells you to fly a kite in—
   - **(A) an open spot**
   - **(B) a busy city**
   - **(C) the water**

---

2. Never use metal wire or—
   - **(A) wet string**
   - **(B) red ribbon**
   - **(C) rubber bands**

---

3. A kite caught in or near power lines should be—
   - **(A) left alone**
   - **(B) pulled loose**
   - **(C) shot at**

---

4. You should call your—
   - **(A) fire department**
   - **(B) police department**
   - **(C) electric power company**

GETTING THE MAIN IDEA

Read the stories, then, on the opposite page, circle the letter choice for the sentence that tells the main idea of the story.

1.   A starfish can open a clam. It can do so without breaking the shells. It wraps its arms around the clam and keeps pulling and pulling. At last the clam is worn out. Its shells open. Then—dinner time for the starfish!

2.   You have seen smoke. It comes from fires. You have seen fog. It's just a cloud on the ground. Smog is a little of both—some smoke and some fog. We take the first two letters from *smoke* and the last two letters from *fog*. That gives us *smog*.

3.   Some people say that a bear squeezes its enemy to death with the famous "bear hug." This is not true. A bear strikes its enemy with its front paws. Sometimes bears also use their claws and teeth. Most often one stroke of the paw is enough.

4.   Do you know how to tell that a boat or an airplane is in trouble? Look for smoke. The smoke signal may be gray or it may be red. The smoke means that the airplane or boat is in trouble. It means that someone must come to help right away.

5.   Sometimes a person who can't have a pet, or who doesn't have brothers and sisters, gets special toys to be his or her friends. A toy puppy that can bark or a soft doll to hug can be company for the person who is alone.

GETTING THE MAIN IDEA

1. The story tells mainly—
   - **(A) why starfish like the taste of clams**
   - **(B) how starfish open clams**
   - **(C) what clams are like**

2. The story tells mainly—
   - **(A) how we get the word *smog***
   - **(B) what fog is like**
   - **(C) why we get smoke**

3. The story tells mainly—
   - **(A) why bears like to hug people**
   - **(B) why a bear uses its teeth**
   - **(C) how a bear fights**

4. The story tells mainly—
   - **(A) what a smoke signal means**
   - **(B) why boats are in trouble**
   - **(C) where to find trouble**

5. The story tells mainly—
   - **(A) why some people can't have pets**
   - **(B) why someone might want a special toy**
   - **(C) what makes a toy puppy bark**

DRAWING CONCLUSIONS

Read the short stories, then, on the opposite page, circle the letter choice that describes something you can tell from the information in the story. Use clues in each story to draw a conclusion to find the correct answer.

1.　　Young birds don't seem to know what to eat. They will peck at anything. Put a stick near them and they will open their mouths and beg. Their mothers and fathers show them what to eat by picking up food and dropping it in front of them.

2.　　How would you like to see everything upside down? It might be fun for just a little while. There are glasses that make everything look upside down. The glasses were made so that people can learn more about the eyes and just how the brain helps the eyes see.

3.　　Baby robins never stop eating. They are always hungry. They keep the mother and father robin busy bringing them worms. During a single day, a young robin eats more than its own weight in food. It eats fifteen feet of worms!

4.　　Snow helped the American Indians to hunt by slowing down fast animals. It also made it easier for Indians to see and follow animal tracks. At the same time, however, animals were better able to see the Indians who trailed them. Indians couldn't get very close without being seen.

5.　　You probably don't think of weeds as good food. Yet, in Japan, many people use seaweed as a part of their regular diet. Often they dry it and roll it around rice. This dish is called sushi. Sometimes Japanese people eat plain seaweed as a snack.

DRAWING CONCLUSIONS

1. A baby bird is likely to—
   - (A) peck at a pencil
   - (B) never peck at anything
   - (C) eat nothing

2. People who wear upside-down glasses are likely to—
   - (A) get mixed up
   - (B) see no change
   - (C) have better balance

3. To feed a young robin each day takes—
   - (A) less than fifteen feet of worms
   - (B) fifteen feet of worms
   - (C) more than fifteen feet of worms

4. The snow helped—
   - (A) only the American Indians
   - (B) only the animals
   - (C) both the American Indians and the animals

5. People in Japan—
   - (A) plant seaweed for fun
   - (B) think seaweed is good for people
   - (C) eat many kinds of weeds

IDENTIFYING INFERENCES

Read the short stories. On the opposite page, read the sentences about each story. Decide whether each sentence is true (**T**), false (**F**), or an inference (**I**). A true sentence tells a fact from the story. A false sentence tells something that is not true. An inference says something that is *probably* true, based on facts in the story. More than one sentence about each story may be true, false, or an inference. Place an X in the correct box to mark your answer.

---

1. Bob saw a crowd of people in the park. He went over to see what they were looking at. In the middle of the crowd was a woman. She was painting a picture of a small boy. Bob looked at the picture and said, "I wish she would paint my picture."

---

2. "Don't go near that tree," warned Harold. "There are hundreds of bees in it. I can hear them buzzing from here."

   "Don't worry. I won't go near the bees," said Ron. "I learned my lesson last summer when I visited my uncle's farm."

---

3. When it stopped raining, Keisha began walking home. Soon she came to a big puddle in the middle of the sidewalk. Keisha ran toward the puddle and jumped high into the air. When she landed, Keisha said, "I should have walked around the puddle."

---

4. Father gave Jim money to get a haircut. On the way to the barber, Jim lost the money. He didn't know what to do! Then he saw his friend, Frank. Jim asked Frank to give him a haircut. When Jim got home, his father asked, "What happened to your hair?"

---

5. The zoo was going to close at five o'clock. Lynn looked at her watch. It was almost four o'clock. "Oh, dear," said Lynn. "The zoo is going to close in about an hour, and I haven't seen half the animals. I think I'll come back again tomorrow."

IDENTIFYING INFERENCES

		T	F	I

1. **(A)** No one was watching the woman paint. ☐ ☒ ☐
   (B) The woman was painting in the park. ☒ ☐ ☐
   (C) Bob thought the woman was a good artist. ☐ ☐ ☒

		T	F	I

2. **(A)** There were a lot of bees in the tree. ☐ ☐ ☐
   (B) Harold could hear the bees buzzing. ☐ ☐ ☐
   (C) Ron had been stung by bees at his uncle's farm. ☐ ☐ ☐

		T	F	I

3. **(A)** Keisha landed in the puddle. ☐ ☐ ☐
   (B) It had not rained for two days. ☐ ☐ ☐
   (C) Keisha was walking home. ☐ ☐ ☐

		T	F	I

4. **(A)** Jim asked Frank for money. ☐ ☐ ☐
   (B) Jim didn't get a good haircut. ☐ ☐ ☐
   (C) Jim and Frank are friends. ☐ ☐ ☐

		T	F	I

5. **(A)** The zoo closes at four o'clock. ☐ ☐ ☐
   (B) Lynn didn't have a watch. ☐ ☐ ☐
   (C) Lynn likes looking at the animals. ☐ ☐ ☐

GETTING THE MAIN IDEA

Read the stories, then, on the opposite page, circle the letter choice for the sentence that tells the main idea of the story.

---

1. Do you know why snakes stick out their tongues? They use their tongues to pick up smells and to feel things. The snake's tongue is not a stinger as many people think. The snake is just touching and smelling with it.

---

2. If you look at the position of a horse's ears, you can tell what it is going to do. If the horse's ears are forward, everything is fine. If the ears are turned back flat against its head, look out. It is ready to bite, kick, or run away.

---

3. The light from a star has to pass through air in order for people to see the star. Air is all around the earth. As starlight travels through the air, the air moves and changes. So the starlight bends, and the star is said to twinkle.

---

4. Pomo Indian children of long ago had many toys. They used sticks, seeds, twigs, cones, rocks, and shells. They used anything that they found around them. They had just as much fun as the children of today have with the toys they get from the toy shop. Best of all, the toys were free.

---

5. Just how tall are you? When you rise in the morning, you may be a half inch taller than when you went to bed the night before. If you go into space, you may return to Earth one and one-half inches taller than you were when starting on your space flight!

GETTING THE MAIN IDEA

1. The story tells mainly—
   - (A) why snakes bite people
   - (B) why snakes stick out their tongues
   - (C) what snakes eat

2. The story tells mainly—
   - (A) how a horse uses its ears
   - (B) how a horse hears so well
   - (C) what a horse's ears tell people

3. The story tells mainly—
   - (A) why stars twinkle
   - (B) what light is like
   - (C) how fast light travels

4. The story tells mainly—
   - (A) how much toys cost
   - (B) where Pomo Indians bought their toys
   - (C) what the toys of Pomo Indians were like

5. The story tells mainly—
   - (A) how your size changes
   - (B) what to eat to grow tall
   - (C) why you get shorter when you sleep

GETTING THE FACTS

Read the story, then, on the opposite page, circle the letter choice that best completes each sentence about the story.

It's Snowing

Snowflakes look like white stars falling from the sky. But there have been times when snow has looked red, green, yellow, or black. There have been snowflakes of almost every color. Think how it would seem to have colored snowflakes coming down all around you.

Black snow fell in France one year. Another year gray snow fell in Japan. It was found that the snow was mixed with ashes. This made it look dark. Red snow has come down in other countries. When this happened, the snow was mixed with red dust.

Most snow looks white, but it is really the color of ice. Snow is ice that comes from snow clouds. Each snowflake begins with a small drop of frozen water. More water forms around this drop. The way the water freezes gives the snowflake its shape.

No two snowflakes are ever just the same size or shape. Sometimes the snowflakes are broken when they come down. Other snowflakes melt as they fall. All snowflakes are flat and have six sides, if they are not broken or melted. When air is cold and dry, the falling snowflakes are small and hard. If the air is wet and warmer, the snowflakes are big and soft.

Would you be surprised to see snowflakes as big as your head falling from the sky? It happened once in the United States. It could happen again.

GETTING THE FACTS

1. Snowflakes look like—

   (A) diamonds   (B) stars   (C) stones

2. Red snow was snow mixed with red—

   (A) dust   (B) paint   (C) stars

3. Each snowflake begins as a drop of—

   (A) water   (B) sand   (C) dust

4. No two snowflakes are the same—

   (A) weight   (B) shape   (C) color

5. All snowflakes are—

   (A) round   (B) hard   (C) flat

6. All snowflakes have six—

   (A) colors   (B) drops   (C) sides

7. Warm, wet air makes snowflakes big and—

   (A) hard   (B) soft   (C) green

8. Snowflakes have fallen that were the size of your—

   (A) head   (B) house   (C) car

FOLLOWING DIRECTIONS

Read each set of directions, then circle the letter choice that best answers the question about the directions.

DIRECTIONS

There are four words in the left-hand column. To the right of each word are two more words. Choose the one that is opposite in meaning to the word at the left. Circle it.

listen	— speak, hear
below	— beside, above
everyone	— lately, nobody
many	— few, some

---

1. You are to find a word that is—

    (A) the same in meaning

    (B) the opposite in meaning

    (C) very easy

---

2. You are to choose from—

    (A) two words

    (B) four words

    (C) five words

---

3. The word you choose must be—

    (A) checked

    (B) circled

    (C) written

---

4. Is it right?   **(A) Yes**   **(B) No**

listen	— speak, hear
below	— beside, above
everyone	— lately, nobody
many	— few, some

USING THE CONTEXT

Read each set of sentences. In each set of sentences, there are two blanks. Circle the letter choice for the correct word that goes in each blank.

Did you ever hear of a "tiglon"? This strange animal lives in a New York zoo. The father of the tiglon is a (1) _____ . The (2) _____ is a lion. You might guess this by its name.

1. **(A) bell**   **(B) tiger**   **(C) book**   **(D) drink**
2. **(A) mother**   **(B) cup**   **(C) food**   **(D) city**

A rabbit grows its own snowshoes! As winter comes, the fur on the rabbit's (3) _____ begins to grow. This new fur makes its feet much larger and keeps the rabbit from (4) _____ into the snow.

3. **(A) eyes**   **(B) street**   **(C) feet**   **(D) house**
4. **(A) bumping**   **(B) melting**   **(C) growing**   **(D) sinking**

Some farmers raise "crops" of worms. They sell the worms for a penny each. Millions are sold to (5) _____ . The little worm is (6) _____ business!

5. **(A) dogs**   **(B) apples**   **(C) fishers**   **(D) trains**
6. **(A) snow**   **(B) big**   **(C) talk**   **(D) sleep**

There are many things that you can do with apples. You can bake them, make applesauce, or put them in an apple (7) _____ . You can cook them or eat them (8) _____ .

7. **(A) tree**   **(B) pie**   **(C) seed**   **(D) flower**
8. **(A) muddy**   **(B) sandy**   **(C) old**   **(D) fresh**

The firefly surprises scientists. It gives off light but does not give off any (9) _____ Since light usually gives off heat, the light of the firefly is a (10) _____ .

9. **(A) sound**   **(B) darkness**   **(C) heat**   **(D) music**
10. **(A) danger**   **(B) history**   **(C) bird**   **(D) mystery**

GETTING THE MAIN IDEA

Read the stories, then, on the opposite page, circle the letter choice for the sentence that tells the main idea of the story.

1. Jellyfish come in all sizes and colors. Some are only one inch across. Other jellyfish are five feet wide. Some are orange. Others are red. Some jellyfish have no color. Poke one kind with a stick and it will glow. Don't let them touch you. They can sting.

2. Can you picture a flower that is about a foot wide? Can you picture a plant twice as tall as you are? There is such a tall plant with a very big flower. Its yellow petals make it look like the sun. It is called a sunflower.

3. The Bridge of Flowers crosses a river and joins two towns. The bridge has been a place of beauty since 1930, when some women decided to plant flowers on it. Small signs tell the names of the flowers that grow there. Many visitors come to see this colorful, rainbow-like bridge.

4. Snowsville, Vermont, has no bank, post office, or traffic light, but it does have snow in winter. Even though Snowsville gets plenty of snow, the name of the village comes from a man, not the weather. Jeremiah Snow settled there in 1814 and gave the village his name.

5. Some letters of the alphabet are used much more often than others. Some letters we seem to use in almost every sentence. Take the letter *e*. It is used more than any other letter. Of the seven letters used most often, four are vowels.

GETTING THE MAIN IDEA

1. The story tells mainly—
   - (A) what jellyfish are like
   - (B) what colors jellyfish are
   - (C) which jellyfish is softest

2. The story tells mainly—
   - (A) why people like sunflowers
   - (B) how tall the sunflower is
   - (C) what the sunflower is like

3. The story tells mainly—
   - (A) what the Bridge of Flowers is
   - (B) which river the Bridge of Flowers crosses
   - (C) how long the Bridge of Flowers is

4. The story tells mainly—
   - (A) how Snowsville got its name
   - (B) how deep the snow gets in Snowsville
   - (C) why Snowsville has no post office

5. The story tells mainly—
   - (A) which letters are most often used
   - (B) which letters are not used
   - (C) what vowels are

DRAWING CONCLUSIONS

Read the short stories, then, on the opposite page, circle the letter choice that describes something you can tell from the information in the story. Use clues in each story to draw a conclusion to find the correct answer.

1. Look at the colors of road signs. Blue signs tell of nearby hospitals, telephones, or camping grounds. Red signs say "stop" or "don't travel into these roads or lanes." Green signs tell of crossroads or bike trails. Yellow signs warn of changes ahead. Orange signs tell about road repairs.

2. Some birds fly against a closed window. They don't see the glass. If you see a bird who has hit a window, don't touch it. It may die of fright. Let the bird rest. It is likely that the stunned bird will fly away in just a few minutes.

3. Did you know that the horn of a rhinoceros is made of hair? The hair is so tightly twisted together that it seems solid. A rhinoceros can knock over cars and break into houses with its horn. Some rhinoceros horns are over four feet long!

4. In very big cities of long ago it wasn't easy to get a glass of fresh milk. There was only one way to be certain of getting it. That was to get it right from the cow. Cows were driven through the streets and milked in front of the buyer's door.

5. The butterfly flower comes in many colors—white, pink, brown, blue, and yellow. So do butterflies. The flowers are shaped like a butterfly's wings. They are between one inch and two inches wide. These plants must be handled as carefully as you would handle a butterfly.

DRAWING CONCLUSIONS

1. You can tell that road signs have—
   - (A) special colors
   - (B) good pictures
   - (C) bright lights

2. Most birds who hit windows—
   - (A) die right away
   - (B) live
   - (C) later die of a broken neck

3. You can tell that a rhinoceros horn is—
   - (A) curved
   - (B) strong
   - (C) shiny

4. People of long ago didn't know how to—
   - (A) keep milk fresh
   - (B) milk cows
   - (C) buy milk

5. From the story you can't tell—
   - (A) where the plant grows
   - (B) the color of the plant
   - (C) the shape of the flowers

DETECTING THE SEQUENCE

Read the story. As you read it, look for clues that let you know the order in which things happened. Then, on the opposite page, circle the letter choice that best answers the question about the sequence of events.

Gentle Giants

Jan Samuels spends a great deal of her life underwater. Many days each week, Jan dives into the warm, quiet water of the Crystal River in Florida. There she watches these strange animals. They look like giant gray balloons. "Manatees," she explains, "are very strange. They look like cows, but they live in the sea. They're large, but they are very gentle."

One day, Jan slipped over the side of her small boat. She swam across a small bay. She stopped a few feet from two manatees, a mother and her "calf." Then Jan dived under the water. She swam right up to the large manatee. Then she tickled the animal's stomach. Slowly, the manatee rolled on its back and seemed to smile.

After a few moments, the manatees came up for air. Jan swam with the manatees some more. Suddenly, Jan heard a loud noise. It was a motor boat. Signs all around the bay told people that manatees lived here. Boats were supposed to slow down. Someone was not paying attention to the signs!

Quickly, Jan pushed the manatees toward the shore. It was just in time. A boat came speeding past. "That was lucky," Jan said to herself. "Another few inches, and we would have lost you both."

That night, Jan and her father talked about what had happened. "It's people like that who are making life impossible for manatees," said Jan's father.

Jan and her friends started a special club. The members work to keep manatees safe. They make sure that no one speeds boats near the manatees and that the manatees get enough plants to eat each day. Most of all, the members play with the gentle giants. They want the manatees to stay in their Florida home forever.

DETECTING THE SEQUENCE

1. **What happened first?**
    - (A) A motor boat raced through the bay.
    - (B) Jan slipped over the side of her boat.
    - (C) Jan pushed the manatees toward shore.

2. **Before Jan tickled the manatee, what happened?**
    - (A) She made sure they had enough to eat.
    - (B) She played with them.
    - (C) She dived under the water.

3. **When did Jan decide to help keep manatees safe?**
    - (A) after the motor boat raced by
    - (B) when she first came to Florida
    - (C) before she slipped into the water

4. **What happened last?**
    - (A) Jan helped start a special club.
    - (B) Jan started helping her father.
    - (C) Jan played with the mother manatee.

GETTING THE MAIN IDEA

Read the stories, then, on the opposite page, circle the letter choice for the sentence that tells the main idea of the story.

1. Most birds do not sing when it is raining very hard. This is also true when there is a strong wind. Birds do not sing much when it is very hot or very cold. Just before or after a storm, many birds sing more than usual.

2. Arbor Day, a day for planting trees, began in Nebraska in 1872. Most states plant trees for Arbor Day in the spring. In some states, though, Arbor Day is in the winter. Florida schoolchildren plant trees in January—one of the best times for tree planting in that state.

3. The apple is the favorite of all fruits that grow on trees. It is dressed in many colors—green, pink, yellow, and red. Almost everyone likes its taste. The apple can be eaten cooked or raw. It can be grown almost everywhere. There are almost ten thousand kinds of apples.

4. Candy is an old favorite with people. Ancient drawings show that Egyptians made candy four thousand years ago. Romans and Greeks liked candy, too. The remains of ancient candy shops have been found in Roman and Greek ruins.

5. Picture a bird with long, thin, bright-red legs that look like stilts. Now picture the body of the bird. It's black on top and white underneath, and it's about fifteen inches long. Now you know what a bird called the stilt looks like.

GETTING THE MAIN IDEA

1. The story tells mainly—

   (A) when birds sing and do not sing

   (B) why birds like to sing

   (C) when birds sing the most

2. The story tells mainly—

   (A) what is done on Arbor Day

   (B) which states plant trees in spring

   (C) what time of year is warm in Florida

3. The story tells mainly—

   (A) how wonderful apples are

   (B) where apples are grown

   (C) what apples taste like

4. The story tells mainly—

   (A) why people like candy

   (B) how candy is made

   (C) how long people have made candy

5. The story tells mainly—

   (A) what stilts are

   (B) what the bird called the stilt looks like

   (C) why birds have long legs

PROGRESS CHECK

Exercising Your Skill

Directions give you steps to follow. The steps should be given in the right order.

The directions below tell you how to make an ocean in a bottle. The directions are not in the right order. To the left, number the steps in the right order.

_____ Fill half the bottle with water.

___1___ Find a big, clear bottle with a twist top.

_____ Put blue vegetable dye in the water.

_____ Close the bottle.

_____ Tip the bottle on its side to make waves.

_____ Add cooking oil on top of the blue water until the bottle is full.

Expanding Your Skill

Talk about the directions above with a friend or a parent. Answer these questions:

- What things do you need if you want to make an ocean in a bottle?

  _____

- What do you do first?

  _____

- What do you do next?

  _____

- What other things do you do?

  _____

- What is the last thing that you do?

  _____

- What things might happen if you did not follow the steps in the right order?

  _____

PROGRESS CHECK

Exercising Your Skill

Read this sentence. Think about ways you could fill in the blank.

I saw a _____ monster movie.

The word you choose has to make sense in two different ways. It has to fit the **context** of the sentence—what the sentence is about. It also has to be the right part of speech. To finish the sentence above, you need to write a word that tells about a monster movie. The word has to be an **adjective,** or describing word.

On another piece of paper, write the sentence. Use a describing word to finish the sentence.

Expanding Your Skill

Compare your finished sentence with a friend's sentence. How many different ways are there to finish the sentence? Did you and your friend use words like *scary* and *frightening*? These words, which have almost the same meaning, are **synonyms.** They are also both describing words.

Now finish these sentences. Use words that make sense in the sentences and are the right part of speech.

1. Lon Chaney was called "The Man of a Thousand Faces" because he never _____ the same in different movies.

2. The _____ worn by the actor who played *The Creature from the Black Lagoon* was made out of rubber.

3. In the movie *The Wolfman,* a man _____ into a wolf when the moon was full.

4. Lightning flashed in the stormy _____ , and Dr. Frankenstein's monster started to move!

5. Count Dracula was a vampire who _____ many people!

IDENTIFYING INFERENCES

Read the short stories. On the opposite page, read the sentences about each story. Decide whether each sentence is true (**T**), false (**F**), or an inference (**I**). A true sentence tells a fact from the story. A false sentence tells something that is not true. An inference says something that is *probably* true, based on facts in the story. More than one sentence about each story may be true, false, or an inference. Place an X in the correct box to mark your answer.

1.   Lynn was at the railroad station. Her friend was arriving on the six o'clock train. It had been months since Lynn had seen her. Lynn thought, "I like living in my new home, but I miss my old friends, too. Maybe someday I can go to visit them."

2.   Arthur and Chris were going swimming in the lake. "I dare you to jump right into the water," said Arthur. "I'll bet you're afraid it's too cold!"
        "I'm not afraid of the cold water," said Chris, "but I'm not going to jump into it. The water isn't deep enough."

3.   "I hope it rains pretty soon," said the farmer. "If it doesn't, many of my crops will die."
        "You're right," said the farmer's friend, "and I'll have the same problem, too. I guess all we can do is hope that it rains within a few days."

4.   Ann looked into the refrigerator for something to eat. She took out some meat and a bottle of milk. Then she got two slices of bread and made a sandwich. "I should wait for supper," said Ann, "but I'm too hungry to wait."

5.   The guide pointed to one huge skeleton and said, "Those are the bones of *Brachiosaurus,* one of the largest dinosaurs that ever lived."
        "What other kinds of dinosaurs do you remember reading about, class?" asked Miss Barker.
        Several children quickly raised their hands to answer their teacher's question.

IDENTIFYING INFERENCES

		T	F	I
1. (A)	Lynn's friend was traveling by train.	☒	☐	☐
(B)	Lynn had lived in her new home for months.	☐	☐	☒
(C)	Lynn would like to take a trip someday.	☒	☐	☐

		T	F	I
2. (A)	Arthur and Chris jumped into the lake.	☐	☐	☐
(B)	The water in the lake was cold.	☐	☐	☐
(C)	It would be dangerous to jump into the water.	☐	☐	☐

		T	F	I
3. (A)	The farmer's friend is also a farmer.	☐	☐	☐
(B)	It hasn't rained in quite a while.	☐	☐	☐
(C)	The farmer's crops don't need water.	☐	☐	☐

		T	F	I
4. (A)	Ann found meat in the refrigerator.	☐	☐	☐
(B)	Ann drank milk with her sandwich.	☐	☐	☐
(C)	Ann wasn't hungry because she had eaten a big lunch.	☐	☐	☐

		T	F	I
5. (A)	The class had never heard of dinosaurs before.	☐	☐	☐
(B)	Miss Barker was the teacher of the class.	☐	☐	☐
(C)	The children were on a class trip.	☐	☐	☐

GETTING THE MAIN IDEA

Read the stories, then, on the opposite page, circle the lette r choice for the sentence that tells the main idea of the story.

---

1.   Every President except George Washington lived in the White House. After President John Adams moved in, the outside was painted white. However, the name *White House* did not come into use until much later, when President Theodore Roosevelt had the name put on his writing paper.

---

2.   Bird watchers sometimes see birds taking a dust bath. They flutter about, dipping in the dust like children playing in a bathtub. Birds do this for a reason. They try to get rid of the little bugs that are in their feathers.

---

3.   Can you imagine eating only once a year? In one meal a giant snake can eat four hundred times as much as it needs. It can swallow an entire cow. Then the snake does not need to eat again for a whole year.

---

4.   There is a huge stone in Australia called "The Rock." It is also called "The Mountain of a Thousand Faces." People who look at the rock often see it first as a large animal. As the sun moves across the sky, the rock changes colors and seems to become different people, places, or things.

---

5.   Not all sand looks the same. Some looks white and seems to sparkle. Some sand may be light tan, mud color, or even black. Sand will have the same color as the rocks from which it was made. It is fun to see sand under a magnifying glass.

GETTING THE MAIN IDEA

1. The story tells mainly—
    (A) when George Washington lived in the White House
    (B) what the history of the name *White House* is
    (C) when Theodore Roosevelt lived in the White House

2. The story tells mainly—
    (A) why bugs like birds
    (B) why birds take dust baths
    (C) how birds are like children

3. The story tells mainly—
    (A) how much giant snakes can eat
    (B) what snakes are like
    (C) how snakes find food

4. The story tells mainly—
    (A) why one rock is called "The Mountain of a Thousand Faces"
    (B) how stones can look like different things
    (C) where a stone called "The Rock" is located

5. The story tells mainly—
    (A) why most sand is brown
    (B) what sand looks like
    (C) how to make sand look bigger

DRAWING CONCLUSIONS

Read the short stories, then, on the opposite page, circle the letter choice that describes something you can tell from the information in the story. Use clues in each story to draw a conclusion to find the correct answer.

1. Cows have baby cows about once a year. A baby cow is called a calf. After a calf has been born, the cow will give milk for about ten months. If the cow doesn't give birth to a calf, the cow won't give any milk.

2. People need to take in about two and a half quarts of liquid every day. They get about a quart from the food they eat. Fruits and vegetables are mostly water. They get the other quart and a half from drinking liquids of all kinds.

3. Long ago the best road in America was the Boston Post Road. It ran between Boston and New York City. It took George Washington more than a week to make a trip between the two cities. Today, with an automobile, it takes about five hours.

4. When sunfish are born, it takes more than ten of them to make an inch. When fully grown, a sunfish may be over six feet long. The sunfish gets to be over seven hundred times as big as it was when it was born.

5. Basketball was first thought up by a teacher. He needed a game for his students to play indoors in the winter. The teacher made up a set of rules, nailed a basket to the wall, and split the students into teams. Soon the students were passing the ball and shooting for baskets.

DRAWING CONCLUSIONS

1. You can tell that most cows—

    (A) give milk all year long

    (B) don't give milk two months a year

    (C) have baby cows three times a year

2. People get most of their water—

    (A) by drinking liquids

    (B) from fruits

    (C) from vegetables

3. It was a slow trip long ago because—

    (A) Washington didn't want to get there

    (B) the cities were farther apart

    (C) there were no automobiles

4. From the story you can tell that sunfish—

    (A) are big when they are born

    (B) grow to be seven hundred feet

    (C) grow a lot

5. You can tell that the students—

    (A) quickly learned the new game

    (B) lived where it was warm all year

    (C) had played basketball before

GETTING THE FACTS

Read the story, then, on the opposite page, circle the letter choice that best completes each sentence about the story.

The Long Jump

How would you like to jump out of an airplane while it is flying? How would you like to jump without a parachute? A man named Rod said that he would like to try it.

Rod had a plan. It was this. He and a friend would jump from the airplane at the same time. The friend would have two parachutes. He would wear one parachute and carry the other. As Rod fell through the air, the friend would hand Rod the parachute before Rod hit the ground.

The day came to put the plan to work. Out of the airplane jumped Rod's friend, a man named Bob. Right after him dived Rod—without any parachute!

Down, down sailed the two men. Rod put out his arms to slow down. Bob held out the parachute for Rod to take. Rod was too far away. He couldn't get it! Down they went, faster and faster. The ground seemed to come right up at them. Rod began to swim in the air to get to Bob and the parachute.

Rod reached out. The parachute was in his hands. He mustn't drop it! Rod got it in place. Then he pulled the cord. The parachute opened. So did Bob's. Both men began to float slowly to the ground. It was a jump Rod and Bob would never forget.

GETTING THE FACTS

1. Rod planned to jump without any—
   (A) friend   (B) parachute   (C) hope

2. Rod's friend would have—
   (A) nothing   (B) two parachutes   (C) wings

3. Rod was to take the parachute as they—
   (A) fell   (B) rode   (C) climbed

4. The first to jump out of the airplane was—
   (A) Bob   (B) Rod   (C) the pilot

5. To slow down, Rod had to put out—
   (A) his arms   (B) his feet   (C) a friend

6. At first, Rod and Bob were too—
   (A) close   (B) far apart   (C) slow

7. To get the parachute, Rod began to—
   (A) climb   (B) hop   (C) swim

8. Both parachutes—
   (A) failed   (B) opened   (C) broke

PROGRESS CHECK

Exercising Your Skill

Directions may tell you how to mark an answer. These are some directions you may be asked to follow:

number the sentences   put an **X** on

write **T** for <u>true</u>   draw a line under

draw a circle around   write a complete sentence

Read each set of directions below. See if the directions were followed. Next to each number, write *yes* if the directions were followed. Write *no* if they were not followed.

___no___ 1. Draw a line under the word in the sentence that tells **who.**

       You <u>ran</u> quickly.

_____ 2. Put an **X** on the word that does not belong.

       eye   ear   ~~book~~   nose

_____ 3. Circle the words that mean the same.

       (little)   big   (small)   cold

_____ 4. Number these words in ABC order.

       __1__ horse   __3__ cow   __2__ pig

Expanding Your Skill

Look through this book and other school books. Read the directions for marking answers. What are some of the different ways of marking answers? Some directions might tell you to **circle the letter beside the answer.** Others might tell you to **write the answer on your paper.** List four other ways to mark answers. How many different ways to mark answers have you found?

_____

_____

_____

USING THE CONTEXT

Read each set of sentences. In each set of sentences, there are two blanks. Circle the letter choice for the correct word that goes in each blank.

The walking leaf is an insect that has the shape and color of a leaf. It even lays eggs that look like plant seeds. The insect moves along like a leaf being (1) _____ by the (2) _____ .

1. **(A) best**   **(B) behind**   **(C) blown**   **(D) cold**
2. **(A) sun**   **(B) wind**   **(C) gold**   **(D) star**

The sun looks like a huge (3) _____ . But you could never hold on to it. It is not solid. It is made up of (4) _____ that are too hot to get near.

3. **(A) fish**   **(B) bird**   **(C) ball**   **(D) jet**
4. **(A) earth**   **(B) water**   **(C) irons**   **(D) gases**

Gold can be beaten into sheets so thin that light (5) _____ through. Such sheets of gold are known as gold leaf. Just a tiny amount of gold can be hammered into a sheet wide enough to (6) _____ a huge field.

5. **(A) bangs**   **(B) groans**   **(C) shines**   **(D) listens**
6. **(A) pipe**   **(B) cover**   **(C) weed**   **(D) cut**

People in the United States eat many hot dogs every year. If all the hot dogs they eat in a year were tied (7) _____ , they would reach to the moon and back more than two (8) _____ .

7. **(A) rope**   **(B) together**   **(C) loosely**   **(D) away**
8. **(A) times**   **(B) suits**   **(C) dolls**   **(D) answers**

Which tree grows the fastest? A young banana tree can (9) _____ as much as two feet in a few hours. In a few months it will become taller than a (10) _____ .

9. **(A) grow**   **(B) run**   **(C) sell**   **(D) shout**
10. **(A) goose**   **(B) house**   **(C) leaf**   **(D) grin**

GETTING THE MAIN IDEA

Read the stories, then, on the opposite page, circle the letter choice for the sentence that tells the main idea of the story.

1.   There is a plant in our country that doesn't have any green leaves. This plant grows about eight inches tall. At the end of each stem is a white flower. The stem is also white. The plant looks like many white clay pipes. It is called the Indian pipe.

2.   Is it a good idea to use a garden hose to dig a hole? The strong stream of water from the hose washes away the earth, making a deep hole. Sometimes, though, the dirt washes up behind the hose and covers it. Then it's often difficult to get the hose back out!

3.   Our eyelashes help keep bits of dust from getting into our eyes. They act as umbrellas. They help keep rain from getting into our eyes. They also help keep sunlight from our eyes. Eyelashes are like frames. Like frames around a picture, they help to make our eyes beautiful.

4.   Some people don't keep their money in a bank. They hide it in their houses. This isn't very wise, however. The money can be lost or stolen. Money is safer in banks. In case of fire or bank robberies, the government protects people's accounts.

5.   A canary is one of the best liked of all pet birds. Canaries got their name from the Canary Islands, where they once lived. Most canaries are a bright yellow color. But some are orange or red or light yellow. Canaries are not only pretty, but they sing cheerful songs too.

GETTING THE MAIN IDEA

1. The story tells mainly—
   (A) why American Indians smoke pipes
   (B) why American Indians named plants
   (C) what the plant called the Indian pipe looks like

2. The story tells mainly—
   (A) how to use a hose for watering
   (B) why a hose is not always good for digging
   (C) how to turn a hose on or off easily

3. The story tells mainly—
   (A) how picture frames help us
   (B) how eyelashes help us
   (C) what eyelashes look like

4. The story tells mainly—
   (A) why banks should be used
   (B) how much money banks have
   (C) what money is like

5. The story tells mainly—
   (A) what canaries are like
   (B) where canaries live
   (C) how canaries got their name

DETECTING THE SEQUENCE

Read the story. As you read it, look for clues that let you know the order in which things happened. Then, on the opposite page, circle the letter choice that best answers the question about the sequence of events.

Left Behind

Almost three hundred years ago, a tall man raced along the island beach. "Wait for me!" he cried. "I've changed my mind!"

The man was Alexander Selkirk. He was calling to a ship called the *Cinque Ports,* which means the "Five Ports." Earlier, Selkirk had decided to stay on the island. He changed his mind at the last second, when the ship set sail. But it was too late. Now Selkirk was alone on an island in the Pacific Ocean.

The next day, Selkirk walked around the island. There were caves to use for shelter, and streams for washing. There were fruit trees, wild goats, and fish. Selkirk could use all of these for food. However, there were no people. Selkirk was truly alone.

That island in the Pacific was Selkirk's home for over four years. He kept hoping for someone to come and take him from the island.

Finally, a British ship sailed to the island, and Selkirk was saved. He went home to Scotland and told his story. Newspapers told about his adventure.

One man who read about Selkirk was the writer Daniel Defoe. He then turned Selkirk's story into a book called *The Strange and Surprising Adventures of Robinson Crusoe.* In the book, Robinson Crusoe lived the way Selkirk did, with one big difference. Crusoe had a friend, a man called Friday.

Today, you can find the book about Robinson Crusoe in any library. Few books, however, tell the story of the "real" Robinson Crusoe—the man named Alexander Selkirk.

DETECTING THE SEQUENCE

1. **What happened first?**

   (A) Selkirk was alone on the island.

   (B) The *Cinque Ports* left the island.

   (C) Selkirk decided to stay on the island.

2. **When did Selkirk walk around the island?**

   (A) before he called to the *Cinque Ports*

   (B) after the *Cinque Ports* left the island

   (C) before he changed his mind

3. **When did Selkirk leave the island?**

   (A) when the story of his adventure became a book

   (B) after he had been there for four years

   (C) on the day after the *Cinque Ports* set sail

4. **What happened last?**

   (A) Daniel Defoe wrote *Robinson Crusoe*.

   (B) The British ship saved Selkirk.

   (C) Newspapers told Selkirk's story.

DRAWING CONCLUSIONS

Read the short stories, then, on the opposite page, circle the letter choice that describes something you can tell from the information in the story. Use clues in each story to draw a conclusion to find the correct answer.

1.   Long ago, people did not write from left to right, as we do today. At first they wrote from right to left. Then they wrote one line right to left and the next line left to right. Later, most people began to write all the lines left to right.

2.   Babies can cry from the time they are born. It takes them about five weeks to learn to smile. In seven weeks or so the baby can make some cooing sounds. It takes about twenty-five weeks for a baby to learn to sit up by itself.

3.   The coast of Australia is famous for its large clams. It is not uncommon to find clams that weigh one hundred or two hundred pounds. However, the champion of them all weighed in at the surprising total of 580 pounds!

4.   The housefly can fly about five miles an hour. The robin can fly six times as fast as the housefly. The little hummingbird can fly about sixty miles an hour. The duck hawk can fly one hundred and seventy miles in an hour.

5.   "Whip-poor-WILL!" You hear this song often, but you hardly ever see the bird who sings it and who is named for it. The whippoorwill is brown and tan with a big head, long wings, a rounded tail, and tiny feet. Its bark-colored feathers make it hard to spot in trees.

DRAWING CONCLUSIONS

1. You can tell that in time—
   (A) writing lost its importance
   (B) things stay the same
   (C) things change

2. Babies make cooing sounds—
   (A) before they learn to smile
   (B) after they learn to sit up
   (C) after they learn to smile

3. It must be hard to—
   (A) find the Australian clams
   (B) tell if a clam is Australian
   (C) lift the Australian clams

4. A robin is faster than—
   (A) a hummingbird
   (B) a housefly
   (C) a duck hawk

5. The whippoorwill is hard to find because—
   (A) it flies too high in the sky
   (B) it sits very still in one spot
   (C) it is the same color as tree branches

GETTING THE MAIN IDEA

Read the stories, then, on the opposite page, circle the letter choice for the sentence that tells the main idea of the story.

1. Did you know that there is a stone named after the moon? It is called a moonstone. This stone shines back light much as the moon does. When light hits a moonstone, the moonstone shines back a silvery blue light, much like the light of the moon.

2. Some people cannot tell one color from another. They are said to be color-blind. To the color-blind, red and green look much alike. There are some people in the world who don't see any colors. To them, everything looks white, gray, or black.

3. If you live in the South, you may know the fire ant. Its sting can make you feel as if you were on fire. The fire ant can kill little animals and make people very sick. Fire ants have been known to damage corn, beans, and other crops. They first came to the South over fifty years ago.

4. Making a drawing of your shadow is easy. Tape a piece of paper to the wall. Shine a light on one side of your face so that your shadow shows on the paper. Have someone trace around the shadow of the side of your face. Then cut out the tracing. It is called a *silhouette*.

5. One flower has a thin stem. A number of leaves are at the end of the stem. In the middle of the leaves are one or two very thin stalks, each with a small, five-pointed white flower. It is called a starflower.

GETTING THE MAIN IDEA

1. The story tells mainly—
   - **(A) where to find moonstones**
   - **(B) what a moonstone is like**
   - **(C) what to do with a moonstone**

2. The story tells mainly—
   - **(A) why people get color-blind**
   - **(B) what color blindness is**
   - **(C) how to see colors**

3. The story tells mainly—
   - **(A) why fire ants came to the South**
   - **(B) what fire ants look like**
   - **(C) how harmful fire ants are**

4. The story tells mainly—
   - **(A) how to make a shadow drawing**
   - **(B) how to make shadows on the wall**
   - **(C) what the word _shadow_ means**

5. The story tells mainly—
   - **(A) how pretty stars are**
   - **(B) how to grow starflowers**
   - **(C) what the starflower is like**

FOLLOWING DIRECTIONS

Read each set of directions, then circle the letter choice that best answers the question about the directions.

DIRECTIONS

A part of a sentence can answer the question **where.** The word **where** makes you think of a place. Find the part that tells **where** in each of the two sentences below. Draw a line under it.

We went to the movies in the afternoon.

There, in the middle of the road, sat a turtle.

---

1. You are asked to find—
   - (A) reason words
   - (B) time words
   - (C) place words

---

2. The words about a place answer the question—
   - (A) how
   - (B) when
   - (C) where

---

3. The answer should be—
   - (A) circled
   - (B) underlined
   - (C) checked

---

4. Is it right?　　(A) Yes　　(B) No

We went to the movies <u>in the afternoon</u>.

There, in the middle of the road, <u>sat a turtle</u>.

USING THE CONTEXT

Read each set of sentences. In each set of sentences, there are two blanks. Circle the letter choice for the correct word that goes in each blank.

Some people put on masks before they go to bed! They do not sleep well unless it is very (1) _____ . Any light at all keeps them (2) _____ . With their partylike masks, sleep comes more easily.

1. **(A) far**   **(B) high**   **(C) dark**   **(D) cold**

2. **(A) falling**   **(B) awake**   **(C) golden**   **(D) smiling**

Fish called glass fish are hard to spot. They often stay in the shadows of rocks. Because they have see-through bodies, their enemies can't easily (3) _____ and (4) _____ them.

3. **(A) buy**   **(B) cheer**   **(C) cry**   **(D) find**

4. **(A) dry**   **(B) help**   **(C) promise**   **(D) eat**

What are your chances of finding a pearl? Out of every thousand oysters (5) _____ , only one has a pearl inside. Out of every thousand pearls found, only one is worth (6) _____ .

5. **(A) cooked**   **(B) made**   **(C) eaten**   **(D) caught**

6. **(A) little**   **(B) money**   **(C) painting**   **(D) nothing**

The giraffe is easily the tallest of all animals. Some giraffes may (7) _____ a height of eighteen feet. Their great height is largely due to their long (8) _____ and long necks.

7. **(A) grab**   **(B) think**   **(C) help**   **(D) reach**

8. **(A) eyes**   **(B) legs**   **(C) colors**   **(D) times**

Have you ever seen a pancake race? In this race people carry (9) _____ . The person who runs the race in the fastest time is the (10) _____ .

9. **(A) bugs**   **(B) balloons**   **(C) trucks**   **(D) pancakes**

10. **(A) picnic**   **(B) winner**   **(C) loser**   **(D) coat**

IDENTIFYING INFERENCES

Read the short stories. On the opposite page, read the sentences about each story. Decide whether each sentence is true (**T**), false (**F**), or an inference (**I**). A true sentence tells a fact from the story. A false sentence tells something that is not true. An inference says something that is *probably* true, based on facts in the story. More than one sentence about each story may be true, false, or an inference. Place an X in the correct box to mark your answer.

1. "Do you have a pair of scissors?" asked Kenji. "I want to cut the rope around this box." Father gave Kenji a pair of scissors. A few minutes later, Kenji asked, "Do you have a knife I can borrow?"

   Father said, "I thought you'd be asking for a knife."

2. "I have to go to the dentist," said Chris. "I haven't had my teeth cleaned in almost a year!" Chris called her dentist on the telephone. The dentist told her he could clean her teeth the next Monday. Chris said she would be at his office on Monday.

3. Maria wasn't feeling well, so she went to a doctor. The doctor told Maria that she had a bad cold. He gave her medicine to take and told her to stay in bed. Maria did what the doctor told her to do. In two days, Maria felt much better.

4. "I always eat popcorn when I go to the movies," said Grandfather. "I've been eating popcorn at the movies since I was a little boy."

   "I like popcorn," said Erica, "but I like to eat candy at the movies. This afternoon you can eat popcorn and I'll eat candy."

5. "May I borrow three dollars to buy a book about dolphins?" Tyler asked his cousin. Tyler took the money and went into the store. Then Tyler came out without the book and asked his cousin, "May I borrow fifteen cents more?"

IDENTIFYING INFERENCES

		T	F	I
1. (A)	Father didn't give Kenji a pair of scissors.	☐	☒	☐
(B)	Kenji couldn't cut the rope with the scissors.	☐	☐	☒
(C)	Kenji wanted to cut pictures from a magazine.	☐	☒	☐

		T	F	I
2. (A)	Chris was going to have her teeth cleaned.	☐	☐	☐
(B)	Chris knows it's important to take care of her teeth.	☐	☐	☐
(C)	Chris wrote a long letter to her dentist.	☐	☐	☐

		T	F	I
3. (A)	The doctor told Maria to stay in bed.	☐	☐	☐
(B)	Maria followed the doctor's orders.	☐	☐	☐
(C)	It took Maria three days to get better.	☐	☐	☐

		T	F	I
4. (A)	Grandfather had gone to movies when he was a boy.	☐	☐	☐
(B)	Erica likes to eat popcorn and candy.	☐	☐	☐
(C)	Grandfather and Erica were planning to go to the movies.	☐	☐	☐

		T	F	I
5. (A)	The book cost more than three dollars.	☐	☐	☐
(B)	Tyler's cousin gave him money.	☐	☐	☐
(C)	Tyler wanted to buy a hat.	☐	☐	☐

GETTING THE MAIN IDEA

Read the stories, then, on the opposite page, circle the letter choice for the sentence that tells the main idea of the story.

---

1.   Would you like to have a hummingbird in your garden? Put about four spoonfuls of water and one spoonful of sugar in a very small open bottle. Paint the bottle red. Then hang it in your garden. If you plant red flowers, it will also help.

---

2.   A mouse will eat almost anything. It will eat everything people eat. It will eat things that people won't eat. If a mouse can't find any crumbs or scraps of food, it will eat the boxes the food came in. Mice have been known to eat candles and soap.

---

3.   Overhead windows are put into the roofs of some houses to let in extra sunshine. These windows are known as skylights, and they are very popular in today's homes. It's important to choose the right shape, color, and size of a skylight to be used in a room. Skylights usually make the cost of homes higher.

---

4.   The eggs of insects are not all the same size. Some of the smallest insects lay eggs that are tiny. It would take one hundred eggs to make one inch. The housefly's egg is much bigger. It takes only twenty-five of the housefly's eggs to make one inch.

---

5.   Japan is very mountainous. Level areas for farming are few. Japan can farm only about fifteen percent of its land. But Japan raises almost three fourths of the food needed to feed its people. Farmers combine up-to-date farming methods with improved seeds to make the best use of little land.

GETTING THE MAIN IDEA

1. The story tells mainly—

   (A) what hummingbirds are like

   (B) how to attract hummingbirds

   (C) where to find hummingbirds

2. The story tells mainly—

   (A) why mice like candles

   (B) what mice are like

   (C) what mice eat

3. The story tells mainly—

   (A) what shape skylights are

   (B) what skylights are

   (C) how much skylights cost

4. The story tells mainly—

   (A) when to find insect eggs

   (B) how insect eggs differ in size

   (C) how many housefly's eggs make one inch

5. The story tells mainly—

   (A) what seeds Japanese farmers use

   (B) how Japanese farmers use little land

   (C) why Japan's land is so mountainous

DRAWING CONCLUSIONS

Read the short stories, then, on the opposite page, circle the letter choice that describes something you can tell from the information in the story. Use clues in each story to draw a conclusion to find the correct answer.

1.　Everyone knows what a penny is. It is just one cent. Did you ever hear of a two-cent coin? Long ago there was a two-cent coin. It was used in our country. About one hundred years ago they stopped making the two-cent coin.

2.　Parts of Chile receive a large amount of rain. In one part it rains an average of 325 days a year. However, in 1916 the people there were amazed at the rain that fell. During that year it rained 348 days, an all-time record.

3.　Many Americans show that they are proud of their country by hanging an American flag outside their homes from Flag Day, June 14, through Independence Day, July 4. These people honor their country in a twenty-one-day salute—flags flying every day during that time.

4.　Are you hungry? How about a nice, tasty leaf? It seems strange to think of people eating leaves. Yet they have been eating leaves for a long time. Lettuce was a favorite food for people two thousand years ago. Lettuce is also well liked today.

5.　Bats eat insects. They eat many of them. In just sixty seconds a bat may go after eight insects. Most of the time the bat gets the insects it goes after. Two of every eight insects the bat chases may get away if they are lucky.

DRAWING CONCLUSIONS

1. You can tell that coins—
   - (A) may change
   - (B) never change
   - (C) are all the same

2. In parts of Chile it rains—
   - (A) every day
   - (B) almost every day
   - (C) every other day

3. The twenty-one-day salute—
   - (A) happens once a year
   - (B) takes place twice a year
   - (C) happens in the fall

4. You can tell that people's taste—
   - (A) always changes
   - (B) doesn't always change
   - (C) is bad

5. You can tell that insects have—
   - (A) an even chance to get away
   - (B) less than an even chance to get away
   - (C) no chance to get away

GETTING THE FACTS

Read the story, then, on the opposite page, circle the letter choice that best completes each sentence about the story.

Who Thought of It First?

Think of basketball and freeze-dried food. Think of waterproof clothing. These are all modern-day items. But they originally came from Native American people.

The Maya people of Mexico and Central America played an early form of basketball. Their "hoop" was made of stone. The opening was set at a right angle to the ground, like a window in a house. The opening was much higher than today's hoops.

The Native Americans of the Andes mountains in Peru were skilled farmers. They grew more than 3,000 kinds of potatoes. The potatoes came in many different sizes and colors. Today the U.S. grows only about 20 different kinds of potatoes.

The Andean Indians also developed a method to freeze-dry potatoes. First, they left potatoes out in the freezing night air. The next day the sun would melt the potatoes. People would walk over them as they melted, to press out the water. This process was repeated several times. When the potatoes were fully dried, they were stored for later use. Just add water and cook!

You are very grateful for your waterproof slicker on a rainy day. The Andean Indians invented an early method of waterproofing. They took sap from rubber trees and heated it. Soon the sap became strong and flexible. Then the Andeans made clothing coated with the rubber to keep off the rain. They also made rubber-soled shoes and balls for playing games.

GETTING THE FACTS

1. The Maya people invented an early form of—

   (A) baseball   **(B) swimming**   (C) basketball

2. Compared to the game today, the Maya hoop was set very—

   (A) low   **(B) high**   **(C) far**

3. The Andean Indians grew many kinds of—

   (A) tomatoes   **(B) potatoes**   **(C) trees**

4. To be prepared for storage, potatoes were left out to—

   (A) freeze   **(B) cook**   **(C) grow**

5. People would walk on the potatoes as they—

   (A) froze   **(B) melted**   **(C) rotted**

6. Sap from rubber trees was—

   (A) heated   **(B) eaten**   **(C) stored**

7. This process made the rubber—

   (A) soft   **(B) smelly**   **(C) strong**

8. With the rubber, Andean Indians made balls and—

   (A) hats   **(B) jewelry**   **(C) shoes**

FOLLOWING DIRECTIONS

Read each set of directions, then circle the letter choice that best answers the question about the directions.

DIRECTIONS

Do things float better in salt water?

EXPERIMENT

Put an egg into a glass. Then pour in fresh water. The egg will stay on the bottom of the glass. Now pour salt into the water. The egg will rise to the surface.

1. You are to find out what happens to things that float in—
    - (A) salt water
    - (B) air
    - (C) a glass

2. Before you pour in the salt,—
    - (A) put in an egg
    - (B) take out the egg
    - (C) pour out the water

3. When a boat is taken from fresh water and placed in the ocean, it will float—
    - (A) worse
    - (B) better
    - (C) the same

4. In the Great Salt Lake, which is much saltier than the ocean, it is almost impossible to—
    - (A) sink
    - (B) float
    - (C) walk

USING THE CONTEXT

Read each set of sentences. In each set of sentences, there are two blanks. Circle the letter choice for the correct word that goes in each blank.

Many people get sick in moving boats, cars, or (1) _____ . The sudden changing from one place to another upsets their heads and stomachs. People who move their whole (2) _____ , instead of just their heads, usually don't get sick on a trip.

1. **(A) phones**   **(B) noise**   **(C) shovels**   **(D) planes**
2. **(A) houses**   **(B) garages**   **(C) bridges**   **(D) bodies**

The walking tree is found in Florida. This tree puts out leglike roots, one after another, and slowly walks toward the water. The new (3) _____ take hold upon the sea (4) _____ .

3. **(A) skies**   **(B) roots**   **(C) cars**   **(D) cooks**
4. **(A) bottom**   **(B) help**   **(C) story**   **(D) book**

The bird called the ostrich cannot fly. But how it can run! At top speed each step of the bird is the length of a bus. Its short wings help (5) _____ its (6) _____ from the ground.

5. **(A) lift**   **(B) kiss**   **(C) buy**   **(D) tell**
6. **(A) weight**   **(B) school**   **(C) noise**   **(D) color**

A box in Georgia will not be opened for six thousand years. The large box is filled with books, films, and all sorts of everyday objects. It will give people of (7) _____ ages an idea of how we (8) _____ .

7. **(A) today**   **(B) rain**   **(C) future**   **(D) boat**
8. **(A) lived**   **(B) stopped**   **(C) sang**   **(D) laugh**

Ants tap the soil in front of them as they walk. If the feelers (9) _____ a seed, the ant picks it up. The feelers help the ant find its (10) _____ .

9. **(A) call**   **(B) tell**   **(C) start**   **(D) touch**
10. **(A) coat**   **(B) legs**   **(C) food**   **(D) ring**

GETTING THE MAIN IDEA

Read the stories, then, on the opposite page, circle the letter choice for the sentence that tells the main idea of the story.

1.   Many roads have long histories. Some roads began as paths for people or cows and horses. Then carriages and early cars used them. Some of these old dirt roads were paved and became modern roads. Some are even highways now.

2.   One kind of starfish is called a sun star. It may have seven or more rays. The rays look like the lines around the sun. This starfish grows to be over twelve inches wide. Like the setting sun, it is also red.

3.   The blue whale is the largest creature that ever lived. It is also the most powerful animal in the world. The blue whale can pull as much weight as four hundred people pulling together at the same time. It can even pull more than a powerful train engine.

4.   Why do people want to jump from airplanes? Why do they take the chance? They don't know for sure that their parachute will open. Parachute jumpers say that falling through space is just lots of fun. They say they jump for the thrill of it.

5.   Sometimes bells are used to scare away birds. Bells warn ships of danger. Bells let us know that someone is at the door. Bells tell us that someone wants to talk to us on the phone. They tell us that a school day is over.

GETTING THE MAIN IDEA

1. The story tells mainly—
   - (A) what the history of some roads is
   - (B) what dirt roads were like
   - (C) how highways are built today

2. The story tells mainly—
   - (A) how many rays the starfish has
   - (B) why children like starfish
   - (C) how one starfish is like the sun

3. The story tells mainly—
   - (A) how strong the blue whale is
   - (B) where the blue whale lives
   - (C) what the blue whale eats

4. The story tells mainly—
   - (A) why people make parachute jumps
   - (B) how fast people fall
   - (C) why jumping isn't dangerous

5. The story tells mainly—
   - (A) how bells help birds
   - (B) what bells are like
   - (C) how bells help people

DETECTING THE SEQUENCE

Read the story. As you read it, look for clues that let you know the order in which things happened. Then, on the opposite page, circle the letter choice that best answers the question about the sequence of events.

Hard to Get

A large bird circles overhead. The bird is a hawk. Suddenly, the hawk drops from the sky. It has seen an animal it wants to catch. The animal gets away, though. Do you know why? It's because the animal is a prairie dog.

A prairie dog is about the size of a rabbit. Its body is brown and a little like a squirrel's. Prairie dogs live in groups called villages. Their homes are holes in the ground called burrows. The prairie dogs dig the burrows themselves.

One of the best things about prairie dogs is their alarm system. A prairie dog spends a lot of time sitting at the opening of its burrow. While sitting, it watches and listens. Then, at the first sign of an enemy, like the hawk, the prairie dog barks.

When one prairie dog barks, other prairie dogs join in. When the hawk dives, it is no surprise to the prairie dogs. They all have warned each other. They wait until the last second, as if playing a game. Then they disappear into their burrows. Finally, the hawk flies away.

Prairie dogs don't always escape danger, however. Coyotes, which are like wild dogs, hunt prairie dogs. Two coyotes will hunt together and trick the prairie dogs. First, one coyote hides. Next, the other coyote trots through the village of the prairie dogs. After the prairie dogs dive into their holes, the hidden coyote comes out quietly. Then it sneaks up close to a burrow and lies there.

When the prairie dogs cannot hear the coyote moving, they poke their heads out of their burrows. The quiet coyote waits near a burrow. It grabs a prairie dog. This is one time that the alarm system of the prairie dog doesn't work.

DETECTING THE SEQUENCE

1. **What happens first?**

   (A) The prairie dog gets away.

   (B) The hawk dives to the ground.

   (C) The hawk circles in the sky.

2. **Which of these things happens last?**

   (A) The prairie dogs watch and listen.

   (B) The prairie dogs disappear into their holes.

   (C) The prairie dogs bark a warning.

3. **When does the hidden coyote come out quietly?**

   (A) before the other coyote trots through the village

   (B) as the other coyote trots through the village

   (C) after the prairie dogs dive into their holes

4. **What happens last?**

   (A) The coyote grabs a prairie dog.

   (B) The coyote waits by a burrow.

   (C) The prairie dogs decide all is clear.

DRAWING CONCLUSIONS

Read the short stories, then, on the opposite page, circle the letter choice that describes something you can tell from the information in the story. Use clues in each story to draw a conclusion to find the correct answer.

1.   The first people to make correct maps were the Egyptians. Before a map can be drawn, land must be measured. The Egyptians made tools for this purpose. They measured the entire land with special measuring chains.

2.   Did you know that "people years" and "dog years" are not the same? Scientists have made up a way to show how much faster a dog's life goes by than a person's. For each "people year," or real year, they count seven "dog years." When a dog is only ten real years old, it is entering old age at seventy "dog years."

3.   Not every letter that is sent goes to the right person. Sometimes the writing is so poor that it can't be read. Sometimes the address isn't right. Each year millions of letters never get to the places the writers wanted them to go to because of mistakes and poor writing.

4.   It is said that people should take a lesson from the clock. The clock passes the time by keeping its hands busy. People who do what the clock does also pass the time by keeping their hands busy and not by sleeping the time away.

5.   A horseshoe crab is often called a king crab, but it isn't a crab at all. The front part of the horseshoe crab is shaped like a horseshoe. A long tail helps it move along the shore. Maybe you have seen the marks it leaves on the beach.

DRAWING CONCLUSIONS

1. You can tell that the very first mapmakers—
   - (A) used a lot of skill
   - (B) guessed a lot
   - (C) knew a lot about chains

2. You can tell that—
   - (A) usually people live longer than dogs
   - (B) dogs and people live the same number of real years
   - (C) dogs live seven times longer than people

3. You can tell that—
   - (A) everyone writes clearly
   - (B) penmanship isn't important
   - (C) people make careless mistakes

4. You can tell that busy people—
   - (A) sleep the time away
   - (B) don't do what clocks do
   - (C) act like clocks

5. The horseshoe crab probably gets its name from its—
   - (A) mother
   - (B) shape
   - (C) color

IDENTIFYING INFERENCES

Read the short stories. On the opposite page, read the sentences about each story. Decide whether each sentence is true (**T**), false (**F**), or an inference (**I**). A true sentence tells a fact from the story. A false sentence tells something that is not true. An inference says something that is *probably* true, based on facts in the story. More than one sentence about each story may be true, false, or an inference. Place an X in the correct box to mark your answer.

1.   Maria got a bicycle for her birthday. "I hope I don't make a mistake," said Maria. "This is the first time that I've ever put a bike together."

    Later, her friend Chris saw Maria's bicycle. Chris asked, "Will you help me put my new bike together?"

2.   It had snowed during the night, and the streets were icy. Mr. Ashman drove his car slowly. He didn't want to have an accident. Suddenly, a dog ran into the street. Mr. Ashman put on the brakes. It was a good thing that he hadn't been driving faster.

3.   Lynn had been invited to a costume party. There was going to be a prize for the funniest costume. Lynn went as a clown. When she got to the party, she looked at what the others were wearing. Lynn said, "I guess a lot of people think a clown's costume is funny."

4.   "There was a terrible fire in the forest last week," said Ashley. "Nearly half of the trees burned down. I wonder how the fire got started."

    "It was started by lightning," said Kayla. "Do you remember the storm that woke everyone up in the middle of the night?"

5.   Jacob heard a motor running. "Maybe my mother is home from work," he thought. Jacob ran out of the house, but his mother's car was nowhere in sight. The motor he had heard was coming from next door. His neighbor was cutting the lawn.

IDENTIFYING INFERENCES

		T	F	I
1. (A)	Chris had a new bicycle.	☒	☐	☐
(B)	Maria had put many bicycles together.	☐	☒	☐
(C)	Maria did a good job of putting her bicycle together.	☐	☐	☒

		T	F	I
2. (A)	The car didn't hit the dog.	☐	☐	☐
(B)	Mr. Ashman is a good driver.	☐	☐	☐
(C)	Mr. Ashman doesn't have a car.	☐	☐	☐

		T	F	I
3. (A)	Lynn had been asked to go to a party.	☐	☐	☐
(B)	There was a prize for the funniest costume.	☐	☐	☐
(C)	Lynn wasn't the only person wearing a clown costume.	☐	☐	☐

		T	F	I
4. (A)	The fire did not harm many trees.	☐	☐	☐
(B)	The fire happened about a week ago.	☐	☐	☐
(C)	The fire was started by a match.	☐	☐	☐

		T	F	I
5. (A)	Jacob couldn't hear his neighbor cut the lawn.	☐	☐	☐
(B)	To Jacob, the motors of the car and the neighbor's machine sounded alike.	☐	☐	☐
(C)	Jacob's mother has a job.	☐	☐	☐

PROGRESS CHECK

Exploring Language

Read the sentences below. Think about how the underlined word is used in each sentence. Then, in your own words, write what the underlined word means.

1. The giant clam is <u>enormous</u> and can weigh more than 700 pounds!

   _____

2. The most <u>valuable</u> shell sold for $10,000!

   _____

3. The long-lived quahog—a kind of clam—can <u>survive</u> for 150 years.

   _____

4. The scallop <u>advances</u> by opening and closing its shell quickly.

   _____

5. Hermit crabs live in the <u>vacant</u> shells of dead sea animals.

   _____

Now write a sentence of your own for each of the underlined words. Think about how you can show the meaning of each word. Put context clues in your sentences.

1. _____

2. _____

3. _____

4. _____

5. _____

ANSWER KEY

NAME

FOLLOWING DIRECTIONS

Read each set of directions, then circle the letter choice that best answers the question about the directions.

DIRECTIONS

Fly a kite in an open spot far from electric power lines. Never use metal wire or wet string. If your kite gets caught in a power line or in tree branches near a power line, don't try to get it down. Instead, call your electric power company.

1. This tells you to fly a kite in—
   - (A) an open spot
   - (B) a busy city
   - (C) the water

2. Never use metal wire or—
   - (A) wet string
   - (B) red ribbon
   - (C) rubber bands

3. A kite caught in or near power lines should be—
   - (A) left alone
   - (B) pulled loose
   - (C) shot at

4. You should call your—
   - (A) fire department
   - (B) police department
   - (C) electric power company

3

NAME

GETTING THE MAIN IDEA

Read the stories, then, on the opposite page, circle the letter choice for the sentence that tells the main idea of the story.

1. A starfish can open a clam. It can do so without breaking the shells. It wraps its arms around the clam and keeps pulling and pulling. At last the clam is worn out. Its shells open. Then—dinner time for the starfish!

2. You have seen smoke. It comes from fires. You have seen fog. It's just a cloud on the ground. Smog is a little of both—some smoke and some fog. We take the first two letters from *smoke* and the last two letters from *fog*. That gives us *smog*.

3. Some people say that a bear squeezes its enemy to death with the famous "bear hug." This is not true. A bear strikes its enemy with its front paws. Sometimes bears also use their claws and teeth. Most often one stroke of the paw is enough.

4. Do you know how to tell that a boat or an airplane is in trouble? Look for smoke. The smoke signal may be gray or it may be red. The smoke means that the airplane or boat is in trouble. It means that someone must come to help right away.

5. Sometimes a person who can't have a pet, or who doesn't have brothers and sisters, gets special toys to be his or her friends. A toy puppy that can bark or a soft doll to hug can be company for the person who is alone.

4

NAME

GETTING THE MAIN IDEA

1. The story tells mainly—
   - (A) why starfish like the taste of clams
   - (B) how starfish open clams
   - (C) what clams are like

2. The story tells mainly—
   - (A) how we get the word *smog*
   - (B) what fog is like
   - (C) why we get smoke

3. The story tells mainly—
   - (A) why bears like to hug people
   - (B) why a bear uses its teeth
   - (C) how a bear fights

4. The story tells mainly—
   - (A) what a smoke signal means
   - (B) why boats are in trouble
   - (C) where to find trouble

5. The story tells mainly—
   - (A) why some people can't have pets
   - (B) why someone might want a special toy
   - (C) what makes a toy puppy bark

5

NAME

DRAWING CONCLUSIONS

Read the short stories, then, on the opposite page, circle the letter choice that describes something you can tell from the information in the story. Use clues in each story to draw a conclusion to find the correct answer.

1. Young birds don't seem to know what to eat. They will peck at anything. Put a stick near them and they will open their mouths and beg. Their mothers and fathers show them what to eat by picking up food and dropping it in front of them.

2. How would you like to see everything upside down? It might be fun for just a little while. There are glasses that make everything look upside down. The glasses were made so that people can learn more about the eyes and just how the brain helps the eyes see.

3. Baby robins never stop eating. They are always hungry. They keep the mother and father robin busy bringing them worms. During a single day, a young robin eats more than its own weight in food. It eats fifteen feet of worms!

4. Snow helped the American Indians to hunt by slowing down fast animals. It also made it easier for Indians to see and follow animal tracks. At the same time, however, animals were better able to see the Indians who trailed them. Indians couldn't get very close without being seen.

5. You probably don't think of weeds as good food. Yet, in Japan, many people use seaweed as a part of their regular diet. Often they dry it and roll it around rice. This dish is called sushi. Sometimes Japanese people eat plain seaweed as a snack.

6

NAME

DRAWING CONCLUSIONS

1. A baby bird is likely to—
   - (A) peck at a pencil
   - (B) never peck at anything
   - (C) eat nothing

2. People who wear upside-down glasses are likely to—
   - (A) get mixed up
   - (B) see no change
   - (C) have better balance

3. To feed a young robin each day takes—
   - (A) less than fifteen feet of worms
   - (B) fifteen feet of worms
   - (C) more than fifteen feet of worms

4. The snow helped—
   - (A) only the American Indians
   - (B) only the animals
   - (C) both the American Indians and the animals

5. People in Japan—
   - (A) plant seaweed for fun
   - (B) think seaweed is good for people
   - (C) eat many kinds of weeds

7

NAME

IDENTIFYING INFERENCES

Read the short stories. On the opposite page, read the sentences under each story. Decide whether each sentence is true (T), false (F), or an inference (I). A true sentence tells a fact from the story. A false sentence tells something that is not true. An inference says something that is *probably* true, based on facts in the story. More than one sentence about each story may be true, false, or an inference. Place an X in the correct box to mark your answer.

1. Bob saw a crowd of people in the park. He went over to see what they were looking at. In the middle of the crowd was a woman. She was painting a picture of a small boy. Bob looked at the picture and said, "I wish she would paint my picture."

2. "Don't go near that tree," warned Harold. "There are hundreds of bees in it. I can hear them buzzing from here."
   "Don't worry. I won't go near the bees," said Ron. "I learned my lesson last summer when I visited my uncle's farm."

3. When it stopped raining, Keisha began walking home. Soon she came to a big puddle in the middle of the sidewalk. Keisha ran toward the puddle and jumped high into the air. When she landed, Keisha said, "I should have walked around the puddle."

4. Father gave Jim money to get a haircut. On the way to the barber, Jim lost the money. He didn't know what to do! Then he saw his friend, Frank. Jim asked Frank to give him a haircut. When Jim got home, his father asked, "What happened to your hair?"

5. The zoo was going to close at five o'clock. Lynn looked at her watch. It was almost four o'clock. "Oh, dear," said Lynn. "The zoo is going to close in about an hour, and I haven't seen half the animals. I think I'll come back again tomorrow."

8

ANSWER KEY

NAME

IDENTIFYING INFERENCES

		T	F	I
1.	(A) No one was watching the woman paint.	☐	☒	☐
	(B) The woman was painting in the park.	☒	☐	☐
	(C) Bob thought the woman was a good artist.	☐	☐	☒

		T	F	I
2.	(A) There were a lot of bees in the tree.	☒	☐	☐
	(B) Harold could hear the bees buzzing.	☒	☐	☐
	(C) Ron had been stung by bees at his uncle's farm.	☐	☐	☒

		T	F	I
3.	(A) Keisha landed in the puddle.	☐	☐	☒
	(B) It had not rained for two days.	☐	☒	☐
	(C) Keisha was walking home.	☒	☐	☐

		T	F	I
4.	(A) Jim asked Frank for money.	☐	☒	☐
	(B) Jim didn't get a good haircut.	☐	☐	☒
	(C) Jim and Frank are friends.	☒	☐	☐

		T	F	I
5.	(A) The zoo closes at four o'clock.	☐	☒	☐
	(B) Lynn didn't have a watch.	☒	☐	☐
	(C) Lynn likes looking at the animals.	☐	☐	☒

9

NAME

GETTING THE MAIN IDEA

Read the stories, then, on the opposite page, circle the letter choice for the sentence that tells the main idea of the story.

1. Do you know why snakes stick out their tongues? They use their tongues to pick up smells and to feel things. The snake's tongue is not a stinger as many people think. The snake is just touching and smelling with it.

2. If you look at the position of a horse's ears, you can tell what it is going to do. If the horse's ears are forward, everything is fine. If the ears are turned back flat against its head, look out. It is ready to bite, kick, or run away.

3. The light from a star has to pass through air in order for people to see the star. Air is all around the earth. As starlight travels through the air, the air moves and changes. So the starlight bends, and the star is said to twinkle.

4. Pomo Indian children of long ago had many toys. They used sticks, seeds, twigs, cones, rocks, and shells. They used anything that they found around them. They had just as much fun as the children of today have with the toys they get from the toy shop. Best of all, the toys were free.

5. Just how tall are you? When you rise in the morning, you may be a half inch taller than when you went to bed the night before. If you go into space, you may return to Earth one and one-half inches taller than you were when starting on your space flight!

10

NAME

GETTING THE MAIN IDEA

1. The story tells mainly—
   - (A) why snakes bite people
   - (B) why snakes stick out their tongues
   - (C) what snakes eat

2. The story tells mainly—
   - (A) how a horse uses its ears
   - (B) how a horse hears so well
   - (C) what a horse's ears tell people

3. The story tells mainly—
   - (A) why stars twinkle
   - (B) what light is like
   - (C) how fast light travels

4. The story tells mainly—
   - (A) how much toys cost
   - (B) where Pomo Indians bought their toys
   - (C) what the toys of Pomo Indians were like

5. The story tells mainly—
   - (A) how your size changes
   - (B) what to eat to grow tall
   - (C) why you get shorter when you sleep

11

NAME

GETTING THE FACTS

Read the story, then, on the opposite page, circle the letter choice that best completes each sentence about the story.

It's Snowing

Snowflakes look like white stars falling from the sky. But there have been times when snow has looked red, green, yellow, or black. There have been snowflakes of almost every color. Think how it would seem to have colored snowflakes coming down all around you.

Black snow fell in France one year. Another year gray snow fell in Japan. It was found that the snow was mixed with ashes. This made it look dark. Red snow has come down in other countries. When this happened, the snow was mixed with red dust.

Most snow looks white, but it is really the color of ice. Snow is ice that comes from snow clouds. Each snowflake begins with a small drop of frozen water. More water forms around this drop. The way the water freezes gives the snowflake its shape.

No two snowflakes are ever just the same size or shape. Sometimes the snowflakes are broken when they come down. Other snowflakes melt as they fall. All snowflakes are flat and have six sides, if they are not broken or melted. When air is cold and dry, the falling snowflakes are small and hard. If the air is wet and warmer, the snowflakes are big and soft.

Would you be surprised to see snowflakes as big as your head falling from the sky? It happened once in the United States. It could happen again.

12

NAME

GETTING THE FACTS

1. Snowflakes look like—
   - (A) diamonds (B) stars (C) stones

2. Red snow was snow mixed with red—
   - (A) dust (B) paint (C) stars

3. Each snowflake begins as a drop of—
   - (A) water (B) sand (C) dust

4. No two snowflakes are the same—
   - (A) weight (B) shape (C) color

5. All snowflakes are—
   - (A) round (B) hard (C) flat

6. All snowflakes have six—
   - (A) colors (B) drops (C) sides

7. Warm, wet air makes snowflakes big and—
   - (A) hard (B) soft (C) green

8. Snowflakes have fallen that were the size of your—
   - (A) head (B) house (C) car

13

NAME

FOLLOWING DIRECTIONS

Read each set of directions, then circle the letter choice that best answers the question about the directions.

DIRECTIONS

There are four words in the left-hand column. To the right of each word are two more words. Choose the one that is opposite in meaning to the word at the left. Circle it.

listen	— speak, hear
below	— beside, above
everyone	— lately, nobody
many	— few, some

1. You are to find a word that is—
   - (A) the same in meaning
   - (B) the opposite in meaning
   - (C) very easy

2. You are to choose from—
   - (A) two words
   - (B) four words
   - (C) five words

3. The word you choose must be—
   - (A) checked
   - (B) circled
   - (C) written

4. Is it right? (A) Yes (B) No

listen	— speak, hear
below	— beside, above
everyone	— lately, nobody
many	— few, some

14

ANSWER KEY

NAME _____

USING THE CONTEXT

Read each set of sentences. In each set of sentences, there are two blanks. Circle the letter choice for the correct word that goes in each blank.

Did you ever hear of a "tiglon"? This strange animal lives in a New York zoo. The father of the tiglon is a (1) _____. The (2) _____ is a lion. You might guess this by its name.

1. (A) bell   (B) tiger   (C) book   (D) drink
2. (A) mother   (B) cup   (C) food   (D) city

A rabbit grows its own snowshoes! As winter comes, the fur on the rabbit's (3) _____ begins to grow. This new fur makes its feet much larger and keeps the rabbit from (4) _____ into the snow.

3. (A) eyes   (B) street   (C) feet   (D) house
4. (A) bumping   (B) melting   (C) growing   (D) sinking

Some farmers raise "crops" of worms. They sell the worms for a penny each. Millions are sold to (5) _____. The little worm is (6) _____ business!

5. (A) dogs   (B) apples   (C) fishers   (D) trains
6. (A) snow   (B) big   (C) talk   (D) sleep

There are many things that you can do with apples. You can bake them, make applesauce, or put them in an apple (7) _____. You can cook them or eat them (8) _____.

7. (A) tree   (B) pie   (C) seed   (D) flower
8. (A) muddy   (B) sandy   (C) old   (D) fresh

The firefly surprises scientists. It gives off light but does not give off any (9) _____. Since light usually gives off heat, the light of the firefly is a (10) _____.

9. (A) sound   (B) darkness   (C) heat   (D) music
10. (A) danger   (B) history   (C) bird   (D) mystery

15

NAME _____

GETTING THE MAIN IDEA

Read the stories, then, on the opposite page, circle the letter choice for the sentence that tells the main idea of the story.

1. Jellyfish come in all sizes and colors. Some are only one inch across. Other jellyfish are five feet wide. Some are orange. Others are red. Some jellyfish have no color. Poke one kind with a stick and it will glow. Don't let them touch you. They can sting.

2. Can you picture a flower that is about a foot wide? Can you picture a plant twice as tall as you are? There is such a tall plant with a very big flower. Its yellow petals make it look like the sun. It is called a sunflower.

3. The Bridge of Flowers crosses a river and joins two towns. The bridge has been a place of beauty since 1930, when some women decided to plant flowers on it. Small signs tell the names of the flowers that grow there. Many visitors come to see this colorful, rainbow-like bridge.

4. Snowsville, Vermont, has no bank, post office, or traffic light, but it does have snow in winter. Even though Snowsville gets plenty of snow, the name of the village comes from a man, not the weather. Jeremiah Snow settled there in 1814 and gave the village his name.

5. Some letters of the alphabet are used much more often than others. Some letters we seem to use in almost every sentence. Take the letter e. It is used more than any other letter. Of the seven letters used most often, four are vowels.

16

NAME _____

GETTING THE MAIN IDEA

1. The story tells mainly—
   (A) what jellyfish are like
   (B) what colors jellyfish are
   (C) which jellyfish is softest

2. The story tells mainly—
   (A) why people like sunflowers
   (B) how tall the sunflower is
   (C) what the sunflower is like

3. The story tells mainly—
   (A) what the Bridge of Flowers is
   (B) which river the Bridge of Flowers crosses
   (C) how long the Bridge of Flowers is

4. The story tells mainly—
   (A) how Snowsville got its name
   (B) how deep the snow gets in Snowsville
   (C) why Snowsville has no post office

5. The story tells mainly—
   (A) which letters are most often used
   (B) which letters are not used
   (C) what vowels are

17

NAME _____

DRAWING CONCLUSIONS

Read the short stories, then, on the opposite page, circle the letter choice that describes something you can tell from the information in the story. Use clues in each story to draw a conclusion to find the correct answer.

1. Look at the colors of road signs. Blue signs tell of nearby hospitals, telephones, or camping grounds. Red signs say "stop" or "don't travel into these roads or lanes." Green signs tell of crossroads or bike trails. Yellow signs warn of changes ahead. Orange signs tell about road repairs.

2. Some birds fly against a closed window. They don't see the glass. If you see a bird who has hit a window, don't touch it. It may die of fright. Let the bird rest. It is likely that the stunned bird will fly away in just a few minutes.

3. Did you know that the horn of a rhinoceros is made of hair? The hair is so tightly twisted together that it seems solid. A rhinoceros can knock over cars and break into houses with its horn. Some rhinoceros horns are over four feet long!

4. In very big cities of long ago it wasn't easy to get a glass of fresh milk. There was only one way to be certain of getting it. That was to get it right from the cow. Cows were driven through the streets and milked in front of the buyer's door.

5. The butterfly flower comes in many colors—white, pink, brown, blue, and yellow. So do butterflies. The flowers are shaped like a butterfly's wings. They are between one inch and two inches wide. These plants must be handled as carefully as you would handle a butterfly.

18

NAME _____

DRAWING CONCLUSIONS

1. You can tell that road signs have—
   (A) special colors
   (B) good pictures
   (C) bright lights

2. Most birds who hit windows—
   (A) die right away
   (B) live
   (C) later die of a broken neck

3. You can tell that a rhinoceros horn is—
   (A) curved
   (B) strong
   (C) shiny

4. People of long ago didn't know how to—
   (A) keep milk fresh
   (B) milk cows
   (C) buy milk

5. From the story you can't tell—
   (A) where the plant grows
   (B) the color of the plant
   (C) the shape of the flowers

19

NAME _____

DETECTING THE SEQUENCE

Read the story. As you read it, look for clues that let you know the order in which things happened. Then, on the opposite page, circle the letter choice that best answers the question about the sequence of events.

Gentle Giants

Jan Samuels spends a great deal of her life underwater. Many days each week, Jan dives into the warm, quiet water of the Crystal River in Florida. There she watches these strange animals. They look like giant gray balloons. "Manatees," she explains, "are very strange. They look like cows, but they live in the sea. They're large, but they are very gentle."

One day, Jan slipped over the side of her small boat. She swam across a small bay. She stopped a few feet from two manatees, a mother and her "calf." Then Jan dived under the water. She swam right up to the large manatee. Then she tickled the animal's stomach. Slowly, the manatee rolled on its back and seemed to smile.

After a few moments, the manatees came up for air. Jan swam with the manatees some more. Suddenly, Jan heard a loud noise. It was a motor boat. Signs all around the bay told people that manatees lived here. Boats were supposed to slow down. Someone was not paying attention to the signs!

Quickly, Jan pushed the manatees toward the shore. It was just in time. A boat came speeding past. "That was lucky," Jan said to herself. "Another few inches, and we would have lost you both."

That night, Jan and her father talked about what had happened. "It's people like that who are making life impossible for manatees," said Jan's father.

Jan and her friends started a special club. The members work to keep manatees safe. They make sure that no one speeds boats near the manatees and that the manatees get enough plants to eat each day. Most of all, the members play with the gentle giants. They want the manatees to stay in their Florida home forever.

20

ANSWER KEY

NAME _____

DETECTING THE SEQUENCE

1. **What happened first?**
   - (A) A motor boat raced through the bay.
   - (B) Jan slipped over the side of her boat.
   - (C) Jan pushed the manatees toward shore.

2. **Before Jan tickled the manatee, what happened?**
   - (A) She made sure they had enough to eat.
   - (B) She played with them.
   - (C) She dived under the water.

3. **When did Jan decide to help keep manatees safe?**
   - (A) after the motor boat raced by
   - (B) when she first came to Florida
   - (C) before she slipped into the water

4. **What happened last?**
   - (A) Jan helped start a special club.
   - (B) Jan started helping her father.
   - (C) Jan played with the mother manatee.

21

NAME _____

GETTING THE MAIN IDEA

Read the stories, then, on the opposite page, circle the letter choice for the sentence that tells the main idea of the story.

1. Most birds do not sing when it is raining very hard. This is also true when there is a strong wind. Birds do not sing much when it is very hot or very cold. Just before or after a storm, many birds sing more than usual.

2. Arbor Day, a day for planting trees, began in Nebraska in 1872. Most states plant trees for Arbor Day in the spring. In some states, though, Arbor Day is in the winter. Florida schoolchildren plant trees in January—one of the best times for tree planting in that state.

3. The apple is the favorite of all fruits that grow on trees. It is dressed in many colors—green, pink, yellow, and red. Almost everyone likes its taste. The apple can be eaten cooked or raw. It can be grown almost everywhere. There are almost ten thousand kinds of apples.

4. Candy is an old favorite with people. Ancient drawings show that Egyptians made candy four thousand years ago. Romans and Greeks liked candy, too. The remains of ancient candy shops have been found in Roman and Greek ruins.

5. Picture a bird with long, thin, bright-red legs that look like stilts. Now picture the body of the bird. It's black on top and white underneath, and it's about fifteen inches long. Now you know what a bird called the stilt looks like.

22

NAME _____

GETTING THE MAIN IDEA

1. The story tells mainly—
   - (A) when birds sing and do not sing
   - (B) why birds like to sing
   - (C) when birds sing the most

2. The story tells mainly—
   - (A) what is done on Arbor Day
   - (B) which states plant trees in spring
   - (C) what time of year is warm in Florida

3. The story tells mainly—
   - (A) how wonderful apples are
   - (B) where apples are grown
   - (C) what apples taste like

4. The story tells mainly—
   - (A) why people like candy
   - (B) how candy is made
   - (C) how long people have made candy

5. The story tells mainly—
   - (A) what stilts are
   - (B) what the bird called the stilt looks like
   - (C) why birds have long legs

23

NAME _____

PROGRESS CHECK

Exercising Your Skill

Directions give you steps to follow. The steps should be given in the right order. The directions below tell you how to make an ocean in a bottle. The directions are not in the right order. To the left, number the steps in the right order.

- 2   Fill half the bottle with water.
- 1   Find a big, clear bottle with a twist top.
- 3   Put blue vegetable dye in the water.
- 5   Close the bottle.
- 6   Tip the bottle on its side to make waves.
- 4   Add cooking oil on top of the blue water until the bottle is full.

Expanding Your Skill

Talk about the directions above with a friend or a parent. Answer these questions:

* What things do you need if you want to make an ocean in a bottle?
  Answers will vary.
* What do you do first?
* What do you do next?
* What other things do you do?
* What is the last thing that you do?
* What things might happen if you did not follow the steps in the right order?

24

NAME _____

PROGRESS CHECK

Exercising Your Skill

Read this sentence. Think about ways you could fill in the blank.

   I saw a _____ monster movie.

The word you choose has to make sense in two different ways. It has to fit the **context** of the sentence—what the sentence is about. It also has to be the right part of speech. To finish the sentence above, you need to write a word that tells about a monster movie. The word has to be an **adjective**, or describing word.

On another piece of paper, write the sentence. Use a describing word to finish the sentence.

Expanding Your Skill

Compare your finished sentence with a friend's sentence. How many different ways are there to finish the sentence? Did you and your friend use words like *scary* and *frightening*? These words, which have almost the same meaning, are **synonyms**. They are also both describing words.

Now finish these sentences. Use words that make sense in the sentences and are the right part of speech.

Answers will vary.

1. Lon Chaney was called "The Man of a Thousand Faces" because he never _____ the same in different movies.

2. The _____ worn by the actor who played *The Creature from the Black Lagoon* was made out of rubber.

3. In the movie *The Wolfman*, a man _____ into a wolf when the moon was full.

4. Lightning flashed in the stormy _____, and Dr. Frankenstein's monster started to move!

5. Count Dracula was a vampire who _____ many people!

25

NAME _____

IDENTIFYING INFERENCES

Read the short stories. On the opposite page, read the sentences about each story. Decide whether each sentence is true (T), false (F), or an inference (I). A true sentence tells a fact from the story. A false sentence tells something that is not true. An inference says something that is *probably* true, based on facts in the story. More than one sentence about each story may be true, false, or an inference. Place an X in the correct box to mark your answer.

1. Lynn was at the railroad station. Her friend was arriving on the six o'clock train. It had been months since Lynn had seen her. Lynn thought, "I like living in my new home, but I miss my old friends, too. Maybe someday I can go to visit them."

2. Arthur and Chris were going swimming in the lake. "I dare you to jump right into the water," said Arthur. "I'll bet you're afraid it's too cold!"
    "I'm not afraid of the cold water," said Chris, "but I'm not going to jump into it. The water isn't deep enough."

3. "I hope it rains pretty soon," said the farmer. "If it doesn't, many of my crops will die."
    "You're right," said the farmer's friend, "and I'll have the same problem, too. I guess all we can do is hope that it rains within a few days."

4. Ann looked into the refrigerator for something to eat. She took out some meat and a bottle of milk. Then she got two slices of bread and made a sandwich. "I should wait for supper," said Ann, "but I'm too hungry to wait."

5. The guide pointed to one huge skeleton and said, "Those are the bones of *Brachiosaurus*, one of the largest dinosaurs that ever lived."
    "What other kinds of dinosaurs do you remember reading about, class?" asked Miss Barker.
    Several children quickly raised their hands to answer their teacher's question.

26

ANSWER KEY

IDENTIFYING INFERENCES

	T	F	I
1. (A) Lynn's friend was traveling by train.			☒
(B) Lynn had lived in her new home for months.		☒	
(C) Lynn would like to take a trip someday.			☒
2. (A) Arthur and Chris jumped into the lake.	☒		
(B) The water in the lake was cold.	☒		
(C) It would be dangerous to jump into the water.			☒
3. (A) The farmer's friend is also a farmer.			☒
(B) It hasn't rained in quite a while.			☒
(C) The farmer's crops don't need water.		☒	
4. (A) Ann found meat in the refrigerator.	☒		
(B) Ann drank milk with her sandwich.			☒
(C) Ann wasn't hungry because she had eaten a big lunch.		☒	
5. (A) The class had never heard of dinosaurs before.		☒	
(B) Miss Barker was the teacher of the class.	☒		
(C) The children were on a class trip.			☒

27

GETTING THE MAIN IDEA

Read the stories, then, on the opposite page, circle the letter choice for the sentence that tells the main idea of the story.

1. Every President except George Washington lived in the White House. After President John Adams moved in, the outside was painted white. However, the name *White House* did not come into use until much later, when President Theodore Roosevelt had the name put on his writing paper.

2. Bird watchers sometimes see birds taking a dust bath. They flutter about, dipping in the dust like children playing in a bathtub. Birds do this for a reason. They try to get rid of the little bugs that are in their feathers.

3. Can you imagine eating only once a year? In one meal a giant snake can eat four hundred times as much as it needs. It can swallow an entire cow. Then the snake does not need to eat again for a whole year.

4. There is a huge stone in Australia called "The Rock." It is also called "The Mountain of a Thousand Faces." People who look at the rock often see it first as a large animal. As the sun moves across the sky, the rock changes colors and seems to become different people, places, or things.

5. Not all sand looks the same. Some looks white and seems to sparkle. Some sand may be light tan, mud color, or even black. Sand will have the same color as the rocks from which it is made. It is fun to see sand under a magnifying glass.

28

GETTING THE MAIN IDEA

1. The story tells mainly—
   - (A) when George Washington lived in the White House
   - **(B)** what the history of the name *White House* is
   - (C) when Theodore Roosevelt lived in the White House

2. The story tells mainly—
   - (A) why bugs like birds
   - **(B)** why birds take dust baths
   - (C) how birds are like children

3. The story tells mainly—
   - **(A)** how much giant snakes can eat
   - (B) what snakes are like
   - (C) how snakes find food

4. The story tells mainly—
   - **(A)** why one rock is called "The Mountain of a Thousand Faces"
   - (B) how stones can look like different things
   - (C) where a stone called "The Rock" is located

5. The story tells mainly—
   - (A) why most sand is brown
   - **(B)** what sand looks like
   - (C) how to make sand look bigger

29

DRAWING CONCLUSIONS

Read the short stories, then, on the opposite page, circle the letter choice that describes something you can tell from the information in the story. Use clues in each story to draw a conclusion to find the correct answer.

1. Cows have baby cows about once a year. A baby cow is called a calf. After a calf has been born, the cow will give milk for about ten months. If the cow doesn't give birth to a calf, the cow won't give any milk.

2. People need to take in about two and a half quarts of liquid every day. They get about a quart from the food they eat. Fruits and vegetables are mostly water. They get the other quart and a half from drinking liquids of all kinds.

3. Long ago the best road in America was the Boston Post Road. It ran between Boston and New York City. It took George Washington more than a week to make a trip between the two cities. Today, with an automobile, it takes about five hours.

4. When sunfish are born, it takes more than ten of them to make an inch. When fully grown, a sunfish may be over six feet long. The sunfish gets to be over seven hundred times as big as it was when it was born.

5. Basketball was first thought up by a teacher. He needed a game for his students to play indoors in the winter. The teacher made up a set of rules, nailed a basket to the wall, and split the students into teams. Soon the students were passing the ball and shooting for baskets.

30

DRAWING CONCLUSIONS

1. You can tell that most cows—
   - (A) give milk all year long
   - **(B)** don't give milk two months a year
   - (C) have baby cows three times a year

2. People get most of their water—
   - **(A)** by drinking liquids
   - (B) from fruits
   - (C) from vegetables

3. It was a slow trip long ago because—
   - (A) Washington didn't want to get there
   - (B) the cities were farther apart
   - **(C)** there were no automobiles

4. From the story you can tell that sunfish—
   - (A) are big when they are born
   - (B) grow to be seven hundred feet
   - **(C)** grow a lot

5. You can tell that the students—
   - **(A)** quickly learned the new game
   - (B) lived where it was warm all year
   - (C) had played basketball before

31

GETTING THE FACTS

Read the story, then, on the opposite page, circle the letter choice that best completes each sentence about the story.

The Long Jump

How would you like to jump out of an airplane while it is flying? How would you like to jump without a parachute? A man named Rod said that he would like to try it.

Rod had a plan. It was this. He and a friend would jump from the airplane at the same time. The friend would have two parachutes. He would wear one parachute and carry the other. As Rod fell through the air, the friend would hand Rod the parachute before Rod hit the ground.

The day came to put the plan to work. Out of the airplane jumped Rod's friend, a man named Bob. Right after him dived Rod—without any parachute!

Down, down sailed the two men. Rod put out his arms to slow down. Bob held out the parachute for Rod to take. Rod was too far away. He couldn't get it! Down they went, faster and faster. The ground seemed to come right up at them. Rod began to swim in the air to get to Bob and the parachute.

Rod reached out. The parachute was in his hands. He mustn't drop it! Rod got it in place. Then he pulled the cord. The parachute opened. So did Bob's. Both men began to float slowly to the ground. It was a jump Rod and Bob would never forget.

32

ANSWER KEY

GETTING THE FACTS

1. Rod planned to jump without any—
   (A) friend   (B) parachute   (C) hope

2. Rod's friend would have—
   (A) nothing   (B) two parachutes   (C) wings

3. Rod was to take the parachute as they—
   (A) fell   (B) rode   (C) climbed

4. The first to jump out of the airplane was—
   (A) Bob   (B) Rod   (C) the pilot

5. To slow down, Rod had to put out—
   (A) his arms   (B) his feet   (C) a friend

6. At first, Rod and Bob were too—
   (A) close   (B) far apart   (C) slow

7. To get the parachute, Rod began to—
   (A) climb   (B) hop   (C) swim

8. Both parachutes—
   (A) failed   (B) opened   (C) broke

33

NAME

PROGRESS CHECK

Exercising Your Skill

Directions may tell you how to mark an answer. These are some directions you may be asked to follow:

number the sentences   put an **X** on

write **T** for <u>true</u>   draw a line under

draw a circle around   write a complete sentence

Read each set of directions below. See if the directions were followed. Next to each number, write <u>yes</u> if the directions were followed. Write <u>no</u> if they were not followed.

<u>no</u>   1. Draw a line under the word in the sentence that tells **who.**
        You <u>ran</u> quickly.

<u>yes</u> 2. Put an **X** on the word that does not belong.
        eye   ear   ~~book~~   nose

<u>yes</u> 3. Circle the words that mean the same.
        (little)   big   (small)   cold

<u>no</u>   4. Number these words in ABC order.
        _1_ horse   _3_ cow   _2_ pig

Expanding Your Skill

Look through this book and other school books. Read the directions for marking answers. What are some of the different ways of marking answers? Some directions might tell you to **circle the letter beside the answer.** Others might tell you to **write the answer on your paper.** List four other ways to mark answers. How many different ways to mark answers have you found?

Answers will vary.

34

NAME

USING THE CONTEXT

Read each set of sentences. In each set of sentences, there are two blanks. Circle the letter choice for the correct word that goes in each blank.

The walking leaf is an insect that has the shape and color of a leaf. It even lays eggs that look like plant seeds. The insect moves along like a leaf being (1) _____ by the (2) _____.

1. (A) best   (B) behind   (C) blown   (D) cold
2. (A) sun   (B) wind   (C) gold   (D) star

The sun looks like a huge (3) _____. But you could never hold on to it. It is not solid. It is made up of (4) _____ that are too hot to get near.

3. (A) fish   (B) bird   (C) ball   (D) jet
4. (A) earth   (B) water   (C) irons   (D) gases

Gold can be beaten into sheets so thin that light (5) _____ through. Such sheets of gold are known as gold leaf. Just a tiny amount of gold can be hammered into a sheet wide enough to (6) _____ a huge field.

5. (A) bangs   (B) groans   (C) shines   (D) listens
6. (A) pipe   (B) cover   (C) weed   (D) cut

People in the United States eat many hot dogs every year. If all the hot dogs they eat in a year were tied (7) _____, they would reach to the moon and back more than two (8) _____.

7. (A) rope   (B) together   (C) loosely   (D) away
8. (A) times   (B) suits   (C) dolls   (D) answers

Which tree grows the fastest? A young banana tree can (9) _____ as much as two feet in a few hours. In a few months it will become taller than a (10) _____.

9. (A) grow   (B) run   (C) sell   (D) shout
10. (A) goose   (B) house   (C) leaf   (D) grin

35

NAME

GETTING THE MAIN IDEA

Read the stories, then, on the opposite page, circle the letter choice for the sentence that tells the main idea of the story.

1. There is a plant in our country that doesn't have any green leaves. This plant grows about eight inches tall. At the end of each stem is a white flower. The stem is also white. The plant looks like many white clay pipes. It is called the Indian pipe.

2. Is it a good idea to use a garden hose to dig a hole? The strong stream of water from the hose washes away the earth, making a deep hole. Sometimes, though, the dirt washes up behind the hose and covers it. Then it's often difficult to get the hose back out!

3. Our eyelashes help keep bits of dust from getting into our eyes. They act as umbrellas. They help keep rain from getting into our eyes. They also help keep sunlight from our eyes. Eyelashes are like frames. Like frames around a picture, they help to make our eyes beautiful.

4. Some people don't keep their money in a bank. They hide it in their houses. This isn't very wise, however. The money can be lost or stolen. Money is safer in banks. In case of fire or bank robberies, the government protects people's accounts.

5. A canary is one of the best liked of all pet birds. Canaries got their name from the Canary Islands, where they once lived. Most canaries are a bright yellow color. But some are orange or red or light yellow. Canaries are not only pretty, but they sing cheerful songs too.

36

NAME

GETTING THE MAIN IDEA

1. The story tells mainly—
   (A) why American Indians smoke pipes
   (B) why American Indians named plants
   (C) what the plant called the Indian pipe looks like

2. The story tells mainly—
   (A) how to use a hose for watering
   (B) why a hose is not always good for digging
   (C) how to turn a hose on or off easily

3. The story tells mainly—
   (A) how picture frames help us
   (B) how eyelashes help us
   (C) what eyelashes look like

4. The story tells mainly—
   (A) why banks should be used
   (B) how much money banks have
   (C) what money is like

5. The story tells mainly—
   (A) what canaries are like
   (B) where canaries live
   (C) how canaries got their name

37

NAME

DETECTING THE SEQUENCE

Read the story. As you read it, look for clues that let you know the order in which things happened. Then, on the opposite page, circle the letter choice that best answers the question about the sequence of events.

Left Behind

Almost three hundred years ago, a tall man raced along the island beach. "Wait for me!" he cried. "I've changed my mind!"

The man was Alexander Selkirk. He was calling to a ship called the *Cinque Ports*, which means the "Five Ports." Earlier, Selkirk had decided to stay on the island. He changed his mind at the last second, when the ship set sail. But it was too late. Now Selkirk was alone on an island in the Pacific Ocean.

The next day, Selkirk walked around the island. There were caves to use for shelter, and streams for washing. There were fruit trees, wild goats, and fish. Selkirk could use all of these for food. However, there were no people. Selkirk was truly alone.

That island in the Pacific was Selkirk's home for over four years. He kept hoping for someone to come and take him from the island.

Finally, a British ship sailed to the island, and Selkirk was saved. He went home to Scotland and told his story. Newspapers told about his adventure.

One man who read about Selkirk was the writer Daniel Defoe. He then turned Selkirk's story into a book called *The Strange and Surprising Adventures of Robinson Crusoe*. In the book, Robinson Crusoe lived the way Selkirk did, with one big difference. Crusoe had a friend, a man called Friday.

Today, you can find the book about Robinson Crusoe in any library. Few books, however, tell the story of the "real" Robinson Crusoe—the man named Alexander Selkirk.

38

ANSWER KEY

DETECTING THE SEQUENCE

1. **What happened first?**
   (A) Selkirk was alone on the island.
   (B) The *Cinque Ports* left the island.
   (C) Selkirk decided to stay on the island.

2. **When did Selkirk walk around the island?**
   (A) before he called to the *Cinque Ports*
   (B) after the *Cinque Ports* left the island
   (C) before he changed his mind

3. **When did Selkirk leave the island?**
   (A) when the story of his adventure became a book
   (B) after he had been there for four years
   (C) on the day after the *Cinque Ports* set sail

4. **What happened last?**
   (A) Daniel Defoe wrote *Robinson Crusoe*.
   (B) The British ship saved Selkirk.
   (C) Newspapers told Selkirk's story.

39

NAME

DRAWING CONCLUSIONS

Read the short stories, then, on the opposite page, circle the letter choice that describes something you can tell from the information in the story. Use clues in each story to draw a conclusion to find the correct answer.

1. Long ago, people did not write from left to right, as we do today. At first they wrote from right to left. Then they wrote one line right to left and the next line left to right. Later, most people began to write all the lines left to right.

2. Babies can cry from the time they are born. It takes them about five weeks to learn to smile. In seven weeks or so the baby can make some cooing sounds. It takes about twenty-five weeks for a baby to learn to sit up by itself.

3. The coast of Australia is famous for its large clams. It is not uncommon to find clams that weigh one hundred or two hundred pounds. However, the champion of them all weighed in at the surprising total of 580 pounds!

4. The housefly can fly about five miles an hour. The robin can fly six times as fast as the housefly. The little hummingbird can fly about sixty miles an hour. The duck hawk can fly one hundred and seventy miles in an hour.

5. "Whip-poor-WILL!" You hear this song often, but you hardly ever see the bird who sings it and who is named for it. The whippoorwill is brown and tan with a big head, long wings, a rounded tail, and tiny feet. Its bark-colored feathers make it hard to spot in trees.

40

NAME

DRAWING CONCLUSIONS

1. You can tell that in time—
   (A) writing lost its importance
   (B) things stay the same
   (C) things change

2. Babies make cooing sounds—
   (A) before they learn to smile
   (B) after they learn to sit up
   (C) after they learn to smile

3. It must be hard to—
   (A) find the Australian clams
   (B) tell if a clam is Australian
   (C) lift the Australian clams

4. A robin is faster than—
   (A) a hummingbird
   (B) a housefly
   (C) a duck hawk

5. The whippoorwill is hard to find because—
   (A) it flies too high in the sky
   (B) it sits very still in one spot
   (C) it is the same color as tree branches

41

NAME

GETTING THE MAIN IDEA

Read the stories, then, on the opposite page, circle the letter choice for the sentence that tells the main idea of the story.

1. Did you know that there is a stone named after the moon? It is called a moonstone. This stone shines back light much as the moon does. When light hits a moonstone, the moonstone shines back a silvery blue light, much like the light of the moon.

2. Some people cannot tell one color from another. They are said to be color-blind. To the color-blind, red and green look much alike. There are some people in the world who don't see any colors. To them, everything looks white, gray, or black.

3. If you live in the South, you may know the fire ant. Its sting can make you feel as if you were on fire. The fire ant can kill little animals and make people very sick. Fire ants have been known to damage corn, beans, and other crops. They first came to the South over fifty years ago.

4. Making a drawing of your shadow is easy. Tape a piece of paper to the wall. Shine a light on one side of your face so that your shadow shows on the paper. Have someone trace around the shadow of the side of your face. Then cut out the tracing. It is called a *silhouette*.

5. One flower has a thin stem. A number of leaves are at the end of the stem. In the middle of the leaves are one or two very thin stalks, each with a small, five-pointed white flower. It is called a starflower.

42

NAME

GETTING THE MAIN IDEA

1. The story tells mainly—
   (A) where to find moonstones
   (B) what a moonstone is like
   (C) what to do with a moonstone

2. The story tells mainly—
   (A) why people get color-blind
   (B) what color blindness is
   (C) how to see colors

3. The story tells mainly—
   (A) why fire ants came to the South
   (B) what fire ants look like
   (C) how harmful fire ants are

4. The story tells mainly—
   (A) how to make a shadow drawing
   (B) how to make shadows on the wall
   (C) what the word *shadow* means

5. The story tells mainly—
   (A) how pretty stars are
   (B) how to grow starflowers
   (C) what the starflower is like

43

NAME

FOLLOWING DIRECTIONS

Read each set of directions, then circle the letter choice that best answers the question about the directions.

DIRECTIONS
A part of a sentence can answer the question **where**. The word **where** makes you think of a place. Find the part that tells **where** in each of the two sentences below. Draw a line under it.

We went to the movies in the afternoon.
There, in the middle of the road, sat a turtle.

1. You are asked to find—
   (A) reason words
   (B) time words
   (C) place words

2. The words about a place answer the question—
   (A) how
   (B) when
   (C) where

3. The answer should be—
   (A) circled
   (B) underlined
   (C) checked

4. Is it right?   (A) Yes   (B) No

We went to the movies <u>in the afternoon</u>.
There, in the middle of the road, <u>sat a turtle</u>.

44

71

ANSWER KEY

NAME

USING THE CONTEXT

Read each set of sentences. In each set of sentences, there are two blanks. Circle the letter choice for the correct word that goes in each blank.

Some people put on masks before they go to bed! They do not sleep well unless it is very (1) _____ . Any light at all keeps them (2) _____ . With their partylike masks, sleep comes more easily.

1. (A) far   (B) high   (C) dark   (D) cold
2. (A) falling   (B) awake   (C) golden   (D) smiling

Fish called glass fish are hard to spot. They often stay in the shadows of rocks. Because they have see-through bodies, their enemies can't easily (3) _____ and (4) _____ them.

3. (A) buy   (B) cheer   (C) cry   (D) find
4. (A) dry   (B) help   (C) promise   (D) eat

What are your chances of finding a pearl? Out of every thousand oysters (5) _____ , only one has a pearl inside. Out of every thousand pearls found, only one is worth (6) _____ .

5. (A) cooked   (B) made   (C) eaten   (D) caught
6. (A) little   (B) money   (C) painting   (D) nothing

The giraffe is easily the tallest of all animals. Some giraffes may (7) _____ a height of eighteen feet. Their great height is largely due to their long (8) _____ and long necks.

7. (A) grab   (B) think   (C) help   (D) reach
8. (A) eyes   (B) legs   (C) colors   (D) times

Have you ever seen a pancake race? In this race people carry (9) _____ . The person who runs the race in the fastest time is the (10) _____ .

9. (A) bugs   (B) balloons   (C) trucks   (D) pancakes
10. (A) picnic   (B) winner   (C) loser   (D) water

45

NAME

IDENTIFYING INFERENCES

Read the short stories. On the opposite page, read the sentences about each story. Decide whether each sentence is true (T), false (F), or an inference (I). A true sentence tells a fact from the story. A false sentence tells something that is not true. An inference says something that is probably true, based on facts in the story. More than one sentence about each story may be true, false, or an inference. Place an X in the correct box to mark your answer.

1. "Do you have a pair of scissors?" asked Kenji. "I want to cut the rope around this box." Father gave Kenji a pair of scissors. A few minutes later, Kenji asked, "Do you have a knife I can borrow?"
Father said, "I thought you'd be asking for a knife."

2. "I have to go to the dentist," said Chris. "I haven't had my teeth cleaned in almost a year!" Chris called her dentist on the telephone. The dentist told her he could clean her teeth the next Monday. Chris said she would be at his office on Monday.

3. Maria wasn't feeling well, so she went to a doctor. The doctor told Maria that she had a bad cold. He gave her medicine to take and told her to stay in bed. Maria did what the doctor told her to do. In two days, Maria felt much better.

4. "I always eat popcorn when I go to the movies," said Grandfather. "I've been eating popcorn at the movies since I was a little boy."
"I like popcorn," said Erica, "but I like to eat candy at the movies. This afternoon you can eat popcorn and I'll eat candy."

5. "May I borrow three dollars to buy a book about dolphins?" Tyler asked his cousin. Tyler took the money and went into the store. Then Tyler came out without the book and asked his cousin, "May I borrow fifteen cents more?"

46

NAME

IDENTIFYING INFERENCES

	T	F	I
1. (A) Father didn't give Kenji a pair of scissors.			
(B) Kenji couldn't cut the rope with the scissors.			
(C) Kenji wanted to cut pictures from a magazine.			
2. (A) Chris was going to have her teeth cleaned.	X		
(B) Chris knows it's important to take care of her teeth.			
(C) Chris wrote a long letter to her dentist.			X
3. (A) The doctor told Maria to stay in bed.	X		
(B) Maria followed the doctor's orders.	X		
(C) It took Maria three days to get better.			
4. (A) Grandfather had gone to movies when he was a boy.	X		
(B) Erica likes to eat popcorn and candy.	X		
(C) Grandfather and Erica were planning to go to the movies.			X
5. (A) The book cost more than three dollars.			X
(B) Tyler's cousin gave him money.	X		
(C) Tyler wanted to buy a hat.		X	

47

NAME

GETTING THE MAIN IDEA

Read the stories, then, on the opposite page, circle the letter choice for the sentence that tells the main idea of the story.

1. Would you like to have a hummingbird in your garden? Put about four spoonfuls of water and one spoonful of sugar in a very small open bottle. Paint the bottle red. Then hang it in your garden. If you plant red flowers, it will also help.

2. A mouse will eat almost anything. It will eat everything people eat. It will eat things that people won't eat. If a mouse can't find any crumbs or scraps of food, it will eat the boxes the food came in. Mice have been known to eat candles and soap.

3. Overhead windows are put into the roofs of some houses to let in extra sunshine. These windows are known as skylights, and they are very popular in today's homes. It's important to choose the right shape, color, and size of a skylight to be used in a room. Skylights usually make the cost of homes higher.

4. The eggs of insects are not all the same size. Some of the smallest insects lay eggs that are tiny. It would take one hundred eggs to make one inch. The housefly's egg is much bigger. It takes only twenty-five of the housefly's eggs to make one inch.

5. Japan is very mountainous. Level areas for farming are few. Japan can farm only about fifteen percent of its land. But Japan raises almost three fourths of the food needed to feed its people. Farmers combine up-to-date farming methods with improved seeds to make the best use of little land.

48

NAME

GETTING THE MAIN IDEA

1. The story tells mainly—
   (A) what hummingbirds are like
   (B) how to attract hummingbirds
   (C) where to find hummingbirds

2. The story tells mainly—
   (A) why mice like candles
   (B) what mice are like
   (C) what mice eat

3. The story tells mainly—
   (A) what shape skylights are
   (B) what skylights are
   (C) how much skylights cost

4. The story tells mainly—
   (A) when to find insect eggs
   (B) how insect eggs differ in size
   (C) how many housefly's eggs make one inch

5. The story tells mainly—
   (A) what seeds Japanese farmers use
   (B) how Japanese farmers use little land
   (C) why Japan's land is so mountainous

49

NAME

DRAWING CONCLUSIONS

Read the short stories, then, on the opposite page, circle the letter choice that describes something you can tell from the information in the story. Use clues in each story to draw a conclusion to find the correct answer.

1. Everyone knows what a penny is. It is just one cent. Did you ever hear of a two-cent coin? Long ago there was a two-cent coin. It was used in our country. About one hundred years ago they stopped making the two-cent coin.

2. Parts of Chile receive a large amount of rain. In one part it rains an average of 325 days a year. However, in 1916 the people there were amazed at the rain that fell. During that year it rained 348 days, an all-time record.

3. Many Americans show that they are proud of their country by hanging an American flag outside their homes from Flag Day, June 14, through Independence Day, July 4. These people honor their country in a twenty-one-day salute—flags flying every day during that time.

4. Are you hungry? How about a nice, tasty leaf? It seems strange to think of people eating leaves. Yet they have been eating leaves for a long time. Lettuce was a favorite food for people two thousand years ago. Lettuce is also well liked today.

5. Bats eat insects. They eat many of them. In just sixty seconds a bat may go after eight insects. Most of the time the bat gets the insects it goes after. Two of every eight insects the bat chases may get away if they are lucky.

50

ANSWER KEY

73

ANSWER KEY

NAME

GETTING THE MAIN IDEA

1. The story tells mainly—
   (A) what the history of some roads is
   (B) what dirt roads were like
   (C) **how highways are built today**

2. The story tells mainly—
   (A) how many rays the starfish has
   (B) why children like starfish
   (C) **how one starfish is like the sun**

3. The story tells mainly—
   (A) **how strong the blue whale is**
   (B) where the blue whale lives
   (C) what the blue whale eats

4. The story tells mainly—
   (A) **why people make parachute jumps**
   (B) how fast people fall
   (C) why jumping isn't dangerous

5. The story tells mainly—
   (A) how bells help birds
   (B) what bells are like
   (C) **how bells help people**

57

NAME

DETECTING THE SEQUENCE

Read the story. As you read it, look for clues that let you know the order in which things happened. Then, on the opposite page, circle the letter choice that best answers the question about the sequence of events.

Hard to Get

A large bird circles overhead. The bird is a hawk. Suddenly, the hawk drops from the sky. It has seen an animal it wants to catch. The animal gets away, though. Do you know why? It's because the animal is a prairie dog.

A prairie dog is about the size of a rabbit. Its body is brown and a little like a squirrel's. Prairie dogs live in groups called villages. Their homes are holes in the ground called burrows. The prairie dogs dig the burrows themselves.

One of the best things about prairie dogs is their alarm system. A prairie dog spends a lot of time sitting at the opening of its burrow. While sitting, it watches and listens. Then, at the first sign of an enemy, like the hawk, the prairie dog barks.

When one prairie dog barks, other prairie dogs join in. When the hawk dives, it is no surprise to the prairie dogs. They all have warned each other. They wait until the last second, as if playing a game. Then they disappear into their burrows. Finally, the hawk flies away.

Prairie dogs don't always escape danger, however. Coyotes, which are like wild dogs, hunt prairie dogs. Two coyotes will hunt together and trick the prairie dogs. First, one coyote hides. Next, the other coyote trots through the village of the prairie dogs. After the prairie dogs dive into their holes, the hidden coyote comes out quietly. Then it sneaks up close to a burrow and lies there.

When the prairie dogs cannot hear the coyote moving, they poke their heads out of their burrows. The quiet coyote waits near a burrow. It grabs a prairie dog. This is one time that the alarm system of the prairie dog doesn't work.

58

NAME

DETECTING THE SEQUENCE

1. What happens first?
   (A) The prairie dog gets away.
   (B) The hawk dives to the ground.
   (C) **The hawk circles in the sky.**

2. Which of these things happens last?
   (A) The prairie dogs watch and listen.
   (B) **The prairie dogs disappear into their holes.**
   (C) The prairie dogs bark a warning.

3. When does the hidden coyote come out quietly?
   (A) before the other coyote trots through the village
   (B) as the other coyote trots through the village
   (C) **after the prairie dogs dive into their holes**

4. What happens last?
   (A) **The coyote grabs a prairie dog.**
   (B) The coyote waits by a burrow.
   (C) The prairie dogs decide all is clear.

59

NAME

DRAWING CONCLUSIONS

Read the short stories, then, on the opposite page, circle the letter choice that describes something you can tell from the information in the story. Use clues in each story to draw a conclusion to find the correct answer.

1. The first people to make correct maps were the Egyptians. Before a map can be drawn, land must be measured. The Egyptians made tools for this purpose. They measured the entire land with special measuring chains.

2. Did you know that "people years" and "dog years" are not the same? Scientists have made up a way to show how much faster a dog's life goes by than a person's. For each "people year," or real year, they count seven "dog years." When a dog is only ten real years old, it is entering old age at seventy "dog years."

3. Not every letter that is sent goes to the right person. Sometimes the writing is so poor that it can't be read. Sometimes the address isn't right. Each year millions of letters never get to the places the writers wanted them to go to because of mistakes and poor writing.

4. It is said that people should take a lesson from the clock. The clock passes the time by keeping its hands busy. People who do what the clock does also pass the time by keeping their hands busy and not by sleeping the time away.

5. A horseshoe crab is often called a king crab, but it isn't a crab at all. The front part of the horseshoe crab is shaped like a horseshoe. A long tail helps it move along the shore. Maybe you have seen the marks it leaves on the beach.

60

NAME

DRAWING CONCLUSIONS

1. You can tell that the very first mapmakers—
   (A) **used a lot of skill**
   (B) guessed a lot
   (C) knew a lot about chains

2. You can tell that—
   (A) **usually people live longer than dogs**
   (B) dogs and people live the same number of real years
   (C) dogs live seven times longer than people

3. You can tell that—
   (A) everyone writes clearly
   (B) penmanship isn't important
   (C) **people make careless mistakes**

4. You can tell that busy people—
   (A) sleep the time away
   (B) don't do what clocks do
   (C) **act like clocks**

5. The horseshoe crab probably gets its name from its—
   (A) mother
   (B) **shape**
   (C) color

61

NAME

IDENTIFYING INFERENCES

Read the short stories. On the opposite page, read the sentences about each story. Decide whether each sentence is true (T), false (F), or an inference (I). A true sentence tells a fact from the story. A false sentence tells something that is not true. An inference says something that is probably true, based on facts in the story. More than one sentence about each story may be true, false, or an inference. Place an X in the correct box to mark your answer.

1. Maria got a bicycle for her birthday. "I hope I don't make a mistake," said Maria. "This is the first time that I've ever put a bike together."
   Later, her friend Chris saw Maria's bicycle. Chris asked, "Will you help me put my new bike together?"

2. It had snowed during the night, and the streets were icy. Mr. Ashman drove his car slowly. He didn't want to have an accident. Suddenly, a dog ran into the street. Mr. Ashman put on the brakes. It was a good thing that he hadn't been driving faster.

3. Lynn had been invited to a costume party. There was going to be a prize for the funniest costume. Lynn went as a clown. When she got to the party, she looked at what the others were wearing. Lynn said, "I guess a lot of people think a clown's costume is funny."

4. "There was a terrible fire in the forest last week," said Ashley. "Nearly half of the trees burned down. I wonder how the fire got started."
   "It was started by lightning," said Kayla. "Do you remember the storm that woke everyone up in the middle of the night?"

5. Jacob heard a motor running. "Maybe my mother is home from work," he thought. Jacob ran out of the house, but his mother's car was nowhere in sight. The motor he had heard was coming from next door. His neighbor was cutting the lawn.

62

74

ANSWER KEY

NAME _____

IDENTIFYING INFERENCES

		T	F	I
1.	(A) Chris had a new bicycle.	☒	☐	☐
	(B) Maria had put many bicycles together.	☐	☒	☐
	(C) Maria did a good job of putting her bicycle together.	☐	☐	☒

		T	F	I
2.	(A) The car didn't hit the dog.	☐	☐	☒
	(B) Mr. Ashman is a good driver.	☐	☐	☒
	(C) Mr. Ashman doesn't have a car.	☐	☒	☐

		T	F	I
3.	(A) Lynn had been asked to go to a party.	☒	☐	☐
	(B) There was a prize for the funniest costume.	☒	☐	☐
	(C) Lynn wasn't the only person wearing a clown costume.	☐	☐	☒

		T	F	I
4.	(A) The fire did not harm many trees.	☐	☒	☐
	(B) The fire happened about a week ago.	☒	☐	☐
	(C) The fire was started by a match.	☐	☒	☐

		T	F	I
5.	(A) Jacob couldn't hear his neighbor cut the lawn.	☐	☒	☐
	(B) To Jacob, the motors of the car and the neighbor's machine sounded alike.	☐	☐	☒
	(C) Jacob's mother has a job.	☒	☐	☐

63

NAME _____

PROGRESS CHECK

Exploring Language

Read the sentences below. Think about how the underlined word is used in each sentence. Then, in your own words, write what the underlined word means.

1. The giant clam is enormous and can weigh more than 700 pounds!

   Answers will vary.

2. The most valuable shell sold for $10,000!

3. The long-lived quahog—a kind of clam—can survive for 150 years.

4. The scallop advances by opening and closing its shell quickly.

5. Hermit crabs live in the vacant shells of dead sea animals.

Now write a sentence of your own for each of the underlined words. Think about how you can show the meaning of each word. Put context clues in your sentences.

1. _Answers will vary._

2. _____

3. _____

4. _____

5. _____

64

The skills taught in school are now available at home!
These award-winning software titles meet school guidelines and are based on
The McGraw-Hill Companies classroom software titles.

MATH GRADES 1 & 2

These math programs are a great way to teach and reinforce skills used in everyday situations. Fun, friendly characters need help with their math skills. Everyone's friend, Nubby the stubby pencil, will help kids master the math in the Numbers Quiz show. Foggy McHammer, a carpenter, needs some help building his playhouse so that all the boards will fit together! Julio Bambino's kitchen antics will surely burn his pastries if you don't help him set the clock timer correctly! We can't forget Turbo Tomato, a fruit with a passion for adventure, who needs help calculating his daredevil stunts.

Math Grades 1 & 2 use a tested, proven approach to reinforcing your child's math skills while keeping him or her intrigued with Nubby and his collection of crazy friends.

TITLE
Grade 1: Nubby's Quiz Show
Grade 2: Foggy McHammer's Treehouse

MISSION MASTERS™ MATH AND LANGUAGE ARTS

The Mission Masters™—Pauline, Rakeem, Mia, and T.J.—need your help. The Mission Masters™ are a team of young agents working for the Intelliforce Agency, a high-level cooperative whose goal is to maintain order on our rather unruly planet. From within the agency's top secret Command Control Center, the agency's central computer, M5, has detected a threat...and guess what—you're the agent assigned to the mission!

MISSION MASTERS™ MATH GRADES 3, 4, & 5

This series of exciting activities encourages young mathematicians to challenge themselves and their math skills to overcome the perils of villains and other planetary threats. Skills reinforced include: analyzing and solving real-world problems, estimation, measurements, geometry, whole numbers, fractions, graphs, and patterns.

TITLE
Grade 3: Mission Masters™ Defeat Dirty D!
Grade 4: Mission Masters™ Alien Encounter
Grade 5: Mission Masters™ Meet Mudflat Moe

MISSION MASTERS™ LANGUAGE ARTS GRADES 3, 4, & 5

This series invites children to apply their language skills to defeat unscrupulous characters and to overcome other earthly dangers. Skills reinforced include: language mechanics and usage, punctuation, spelling, vocabulary, reading comprehension, and creative writing.

TITLE
Grade 3: Mission Masters™ Freezing Frenzy
Grade 4: Mission Masters™ Network Nightmare
Grade 5: Mission Masters™ Mummy Mysteries

BASIC SKILLS BUILDER K to 2 – THE MAGIC APPLEHOUSE

At the Magic Applehouse, children discover that Abigail Appleseed runs a deliciously successful business selling apple pies, tarts, and other apple treats. Enthusiasm grows as children join in the fun of helping Abigail run her business. Along the way they'll develop computer and entrepreneurial skills to last a lifetime. They will run their own business – all while they're having bushels of fun!

> **TITLE**
> Basic Skills Builder –The Magic Applehouse

TEST PREP – SCORING HIGH

This grade-based testing software will help prepare your child for standardized achievement tests given by his or her school. Scoring High specifically targets the skills required for success on the Stanford Achievement Test (SAT) for grades three through eight. Lessons and test questions follow the same format and cover the same content areas as questions appearing on the actual SAT tests. The practice tests are modeled after the SAT test-taking experience with similar directions, number of questions per section, and bubble-sheet answer choices.

Scoring High is a child's first-class ticket to a winning score on standardized achievement tests!

> **TITLE**
> Grades 3 to 5: Scoring High Test Prep
> Grades 6 to 8: Scoring High Test Prep

SCIENCE

Mastering the principles of both physical and life science has never been so FUN for kids grades six and above as it is while they are exploring McGraw-Hill's edutainment software!

> **TITLE**
> Grades 6 & up: Life Science
> Grades 8 & up: Physical Science

REFERENCE

The National Museum of Women in the Arts has teamed with McGraw-Hill Consumer Products to bring you this superb collection available for your enjoyment on CD-ROM.

This special collection is a visual diary of 200 women artists from the Renaissance to the present, spanning 500 years of creativity.

You will discover the art of women who excelled in all the great art movements of history. Artists who pushed the boundaries of abstract, genre, landscape, narrative, portrait, and still-life styles; as well as artists forced to push the societal limits placed on women through the ages.

> **TITLE**
> Women in the Arts

Most titles for Windows 3.1™, Windows '95™ & '98™, and Macintosh™.

Visit us on the Internet at:
www.MHkids.com

Or call 800-298-4119 for your local retailer.

McGraw-Hill
Consumer Products

All our workbooks meet school curriculum guidelines and correspond to
The McGraw-Hill Companies classroom textbooks.

SPECTRUM SERIES

DOLCH Sight Word Activities

The DOLCH Sight Word Activities Workbooks use the classic Dolch list of 220 basic vocabulary words that make up from 50% to 75% of all reading matter that children ordinarily encounter. Since these words are ordinarily recognized on sight, they are called *sight words*. Volume 1 includes 110 sight words. Volume 2 covers the remainder of the list. Over 160 pages.

TITLE	ISBN	PRICE
Grades K-1 Vol. 1	1-57768-429-X	$9.95
Grades K-1 Vol. 2	1-57768-439-7	$9.95

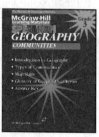

GEOGRAPHY

Full-color, three-part lessons strengthen geography knowledge and map reading skills. Focusing on five geographic themes including location, place, human/environmental interaction, movement, and regions. Over 150 pages. Glossary of geographical terms and answer key included.

TITLE	ISBN	PRICE
Gr 3, Communities	1-57768-153-3	$7.95
Gr 4, Regions	1-57768-154-1	$7.95
Gr 5, USA	1-57768-155-X	$7.95
Gr 6, World	1-57768-156-8	$7.95

MATH

Features easy-to-follow instructions that give students a clear path to success. This series has comprehensive coverage of the basic skills, helping children to master math fundamentals. Over 150 pages. Answer key included.

TITLE	ISBN	PRICE
Grade 1	1-57768-111-8	$6.95
Grade 2	1-57768-112-6	$6.95
Grade 3	1-57768-113-4	$6.95
Grade 4	1-57768-114-2	$6.95
Grade 5	1-57768-115-0	$6.95
Grade 6	1-57768-116-9	$6.95
Grade 7	1-57768-117-7	$6.95
Grade 8	1-57768-118-5	$6.95

PHONICS

Provides everything children need to build multiple skills in language. Focusing on phonics, structural analysis, and dictionary skills, this series also offers creative ideas for using phonics and word study skills in other language arts. Over 200 pages. Answer key included.

TITLE	ISBN	PRICE
Grade K	1-57768-120-7	$6.95
Grade 1	1-57768-121-5	$6.95
Grade 2	1-57768-122-3	$6.95
Grade 3	1-57768-123-1	$6.95
Grade 4	1-57768-124-X	$6.95
Grade 5	1-57768-125-8	$6.95
Grade 6	1-57768-126-6	$6.95

SPECTRUM SERIES – continued

READING

This full-color series creates an enjoyable reading environment, even for below-average readers. Each book contains captivating content, colorful characters, and compelling illustrations, so children are eager to find out what happens next. Over 150 pages. Answer key included.

TITLE	ISBN	PRICE
Grade K	1-57768-130-4	$6.95
Grade 1	1-57768-131-2	$6.95
Grade 2	1-57768-132-0	$6.95
Grade 3	1-57768-133-9	$6.95
Grade 4	1-57768-134-7	$6.95
Grade 5	1-57768-135-5	$6.95
Grade 6	1-57768-136-3	$6.95

SPELLING

This full-color series links spelling to reading and writing and increases skills in words and meanings, consonant and vowel spellings, and proofreading practice. Over 200 pages. Speller dictionary and answer key included.

TITLE	ISBN	PRICE
Grade 1	1-57768-161-4	$7.95
Grade 2	1-57768-162-2	$7.95
Grade 3	1-57768-163-0	$7.95
Grade 4	1-57768-164-9	$7.95
Grade 5	1-57768-165-7	$7.95
Grade 6	1-57768-166-5	$7.95

WRITING

Lessons focus on creative and expository writing using clearly stated objectives and pre-writing exercises. Eight essential reading skills are applied. Activities include main idea, sequence, comparison, detail, fact and opinion, cause and effect, and making a point. Over 130 pages. Answer key included.

TITLE	ISBN	PRICE
Grade 1	1-57768-141-X	$6.95
Grade 2	1-57768-142-8	$6.95
Grade 3	1-57768-143-6	$6.95
Grade 4	1-57768-144-4	$6.95
Grade 5	1-57768-145-2	$6.95
Grade 6	1-57768-146-0	$6.95
Grade 7	1-57768-147-9	$6.95
Grade 8	1-57768-148-7	$6.95

TEST PREP
From the Nation's #1 Testing Company

Prepares children to do their best on current editions of the five major standardized tests. Activities reinforce test-taking skills through examples, tips, practice, and timed exercises. Subjects include reading, math, and language. Over 150 pages. Answer key included.

TITLE	ISBN	PRICE
Grade 1	1-57768-101-0	$8.95
Grade 2	1-57768-102-9	$8.95
Grade 3	1-57768-103-7	$8.95
Grade 4	1-57768-104-5	$8.95
Grade 5	1-57768-105-3	$8.95
Grade 6	1-57768-106-1	$8.95
Grade 7	1-57768-107-X	$8.95
Grade 8	1-57768-108-8	$8.95

Visit us on the Internet at:

www.MHkids.com

Or call 800-298-4119 for your local retailer.

The McGraw·Hill

The Junior ACADEMIC SERIES

CERTIFICATE OF ACCOMPLISHMENT

THIS CERTIFIES THAT

HAS SUCCESSFULLY COMPLETED
THE JUNIOR ACADEMIC'S™

GRADE 3

WORKBOOK.

ENRICHMENT READING

CONGRATULATIONS AND KEEP UP THE GOOD WORK!

The McGraw·Hill Companies

Publisher